The Legion Team
Forgotten Hockey in Waterloo, 1927-1930

Tim Harwood

Copyright © 2013 Tim Harwood
BTSCP Books – Waterloo, Iowa

All rights reserved.

ISBN: 0615829856
ISBN-13: 978-0615829852

Carl Chapman
1914

Fred Becker
1915

*For Lt. Chapman and Lt. Becker
and
all heroes who inspire the best in us.*

Portraits from the archives of The Grout Museum of History and Science,
Waterloo, IA

Also by this author:

Black Hawks Chronicle: Five Decades of Teams, Games, and Players

CONTENTS

1.	Heroes' Heritage	1
2.	A Creditable Sextet	21
3.	Bigger and Better	36
4.	Olympians and Professionals	52
5.	A Service to the Community	76
6.	Pessimism Not Intended	102
	Acknowledgements	128
	Appendix – Game-by-Game History	132

HEROES' HERITAGE

Carl Chapman waited for the snap deep in his own end zone with the Waterloo West goalposts looming over his head. The glum, damp Thanksgiving afternoon was fading quickly toward darkness. West High led Waterloo East 8-3 late in the fourth quarter as the schools met at Cedar River Park for the 1913 edition of their annual, crosstown grudge football game.

Three hundred cars, a sizable percentage of the motor vehicles in the community of nearly 30,000, had carried some of the thousands of fans to the riverfront for the fifth renewal of the series. Steady advanced ticket sales had led to predictions for a record turnout nearly a week earlier. Wednesday evening parades and pep rallies the night before the matchup had brought the pregame excitement outdoors on both sides of the Cedar. Although East had won six of the seven games on their 1913 schedule, West was the favorite in the season finale, with a hard-fought 3-3-1 mark earned against strong competition. Chapman, the senior captain and smallest starter on the old rose and black-clad squad, was attempting to lead his school to a third consecutive win versus East, after the orange and black had claimed the inaugural 1909 game, plus the 1910 rematch.

With only 16 players on his team, Chapman had already spent a busy afternoon gaining 30 yards from scrimmage while running the West offense as quarterback, intercepting a pass on defense, returning kicks, and most importantly, punting. The *Waterloo Reporter* noted the next day:

> Captain Chapman, playing his last game for West High, played the best game of the entire season, being sure on catching and returning punts and showing good head work in directing the play of the team…Chapman got most of his punts away in good shape and placed them so that it was extremely hard for the East backs to cover them…

It had been a game of punting and field position. West had been turned away at the goal line on the best opportunity for either team to score a touchdown during the first half. Instead, East recorded the only points in the first two quarters on a field goal booted from the 25-yard line. At halftime, a donnybrook broke out on the field as the crowd – which had to be pushed away from the sidelines all throughout the afternoon – overflowed. With order eventually restored, West finally broke through at the end of the third quarter; a 40-yard carry by Clyde Davis set up Bill Cotter's two-yard touchdown run two plays later. The extra point kick was no good. However, the ensuing kickoff was mishandled by East, resulting in a safety and giving West their 8-3 lead entering the final period.

East High put together their best drive of the game after taking the ball near midfield halfway through the fourth quarter. Dick Rath caught a 20-yard pass from brother Gordon, the only completion East enjoyed during the day, and the longest of three total receptions in the matchup. Five snaps later, it was first down and goal-to-go on the nine. East picked up eight-and-a-half yards on the next three plays. On fourth down, less than a foot from an almost certain win, East gave the ball to Arthur Simpson who tried to push through the right side of the line. West tackle Ray Gollinvaux pushed back. The ball was turned over to West on downs after the stop.

Now on first down, Chapman was standing far behind the line of scrimmage. The call was for the West captain to punt for the seventh time during the game. It was not unorthodox strategy for the era. Both teams had kicked out of trouble throughout the afternoon when backed deep into their own territory. Although East would regain possession of the ball, it would be difficult for them to rally from the lost field position during limited remaining time, still in need of six points.

The signals were barked out and the ball was hiked back to Chapman. Right behind it came East junior Fred Becker, dashing through the middle of the line. Becker stretched and knocked the ball away as it left Chapman's foot. It skidded through the end zone and the chase was on.

"Both Becker and Gollinvaux dove for the ball," recounted the *Waterloo Reporter*, "and the referee awarded the ball to West High for the latter had had the ball in his hands first. While this play counted as a safety and two points for East High, a touchdown would have been the result had an East man recovered the ball on the blocked kick."

Despite protests by East that they had pounced on the

football, play restarted as West kicked off from their own 20 yard line, recovered a fumble, then punted again. East failed to gain any significant ground, surrendering possession twice more, leading to more quick West punts. The game wound down with Waterloo West on top, 8-5. The victors celebrated, the losing team shed tears, and the *Waterloo Evening Courier* dubbed the affair "the greatest football contest in Waterloo's history."

* * *

Six months after winning his last prep football game, Chapman graduated from Waterloo West High School. During four years of attendance, he was voted class president twice, argued for the debate team, sang in the glee club, and concluded his athletic career in March, 1914, by contributing to a pair of double-digit wins against the rival school from across town as a senior forward on the basketball squad. Born Charles W. Chapman Jr. on December 29, 1895, he was known almost universally as "Carl." Charles Chapman Sr. managed a lumberyard in Waterloo. The family, including two brothers and one sister, had moved west to their new hometown from Dubuque in 1901. Having completed his local schooling, Carl, the youngest member of the Chapman household, departed for Amherst College in Massachusetts during the late summer of 1914.

While Chapman was enjoying the months between high school and college, a tenuous series of alliances a hemisphere away was tugging Europe into conflict. The assassination in late June of Franz Ferdinand, heir to the Austro-Hungarian Empire, led to dozens of war declarations within two months. The Central Powers, including Germany and Austria-Hungary, were pitted against Russia, France, and England. Both sides proved capable of killing on a scale which fit the industrial era. "The Great War" would be the impetus for the invention or large-scale introduction of machine guns, tanks, chemical weapons, submarines, flamethrowers, hand grenades, and more.

Writing in the months following the Armistice in his *History of the World War*, Dr. Francis March remarked, "Never since the dawn of time had there been such a perversion of knowledge to criminal purposes; never had science contributed such a deadly toll to the fanatic and criminal intentions of a war-crazed class."

For Chapman, his freshman classmates at Amherst, and most of America, the European conflict might have been something to talk about, but certainly not an affair to get involved in during its early years. The United States hoped to remain neutral. An ocean insulated North America from the hostilities. As the war churned on however, it became evident that the U.S. would have to choose a side. The sinking by German U-boats of several ships coming to or embarking from east coast ports helped convince America to formally side with the Allies. The United States recalled their ambassador from Berlin early in 1917 and declared war against Germany on April 6th.

Chapman made up his mind to go to Europe before his country was officially committed. He was one of several Amherst students who traveled to France together in the early spring. The group enlisted to become ambulance drivers and stretcher bearers, but it was less than a month before Chapman was convinced to rethink his choice of participation. As the *Waterloo Times-Tribune* later recounted, "…the ambulance corps was regarded by the

French populace as a department for cripples and old men."

From that humble but necessary duty, the 21-year-old turned next to service in which, according to Dr. March, 50,000 men were "…emblazoned with superb heroisms, with God-like daring, and with such utter disdain of death that they were raised out of the olden ranks of mere earth-crawling mankind and became supermen of the air."

Airplanes battled each other and armies on the ground for the first time during The World War. They were a military innovation requiring constant, tireless effort to remain in flight. According to a contemporary news service report reprinted in the *White Bear Press* of Minnesota, a single plane needed a ground crew of more than three dozen technicians to remain in action. "The life of a plane," the article continued, "is not more than two months, and the engine must be overhauled after each 75 hours."

Chapman was promised the opportunity to fight in the skies alongside other Americans in the French Army as part of the Lafayette Flying Squadron. With this unit, he trained to become a pilot in southern France throughout 1917. Manning a single-engine machine, Chapman climbed as high as 16,000 feet above the ground one day and buzzed at top speed just above the rooftops of small towns the next. During exercises, he would dive, twirl, and jerk the open-cockpit machine through the air to demonstrate his control and abilities to flight instructors.

Chapman remained with the French forces through January 1918, still untested in combat. He was transferred to the U.S. Army Air Corps, predecessor of the Air Force, in February. The new assignment brought a commission as a second lieutenant. He expected to be joined later in the spring by his older brother Joe, also a second lieutenant, who had enlisted in the Air Corps and was training in the States to be part of the ground crew. It only remained for the younger Lt. Chapman to be assigned a plane.

Early on the morning of April 19th, he was finally airborne and headed for the front lines. Mechanical difficulties separated him from his two wingmen, but Chapman was able to remedy his engine troubles and continue on. His comrades were nowhere to be found, so the lieutenant cautiously scanned the horizon, as he described in a letter home:

> "Three looks behind to one forward" is an aviation maxim. That morning I made it about five to one. I was twisting and turning, climbing up and going down in such rapid succession that I am sure no German would ever have gotten very close to me without me seeing him.
>
> I was over the lines for an hour, learning the sector and incidentally looking for the rest of my patrol, but I never found them, nor did they see me. The clouds were at about 1,000 metres and quite thick and were getting thicker all the time. I had reached one end of our sector and had decided to go back to the other end and go home. So I twisted back and forth until I thought I must be at the other end but was not sure as the clouds had become so thick that only now and then could I see the ground. At the east end of our sector the line turns from an east-west direction to approximately north-south. I had gone east too far so consequently I was over the German line. I decided to come down to see where I was.
>
> I thought I was south of our own trenches, but what I thought were ours turned out to be boche [German]. I cut my engine and came down through the clouds. Just as I came out of the clouds I head a crack! crack! I looked off to one side and saw small black puffs of smoke which I knew were boche anti-aircraft shells exploding. A second later I saw red streaks

going past me on the other side and I knew that these were the tracer bullets from machine guns.

(Reprinted in the *Waterloo Evening Courier and Reporter*, May 10, 1918)

Chapman kicked the engines back on and launched his plane toward the safety of the clouds. He dodged through the thick air, still hearing enemy fire whizzing around him. Carefully, he made his way home, concealing himself as best as possible. When he landed, both he and his plane were unscathed. The lieutenant had successfully been under fire for the first time.

Luck was with Chapman again the next morning. On this patrol, his challenge was neither an enemy in the air nor on the ground. Returning to base after a quiet flight, Chapman lost his bearings in heavy fog. Coming in for a landing, he realized his descent was taking him to the ground to quickly. Pulling back on the controls, he changed the angle but could not keep the plane off the earth. Crashing beside the runway, Chapman's plane flipped tail-over-propeller, wrecking it, but leaving him with only a blackened eye. Since it was common for aircraft to meet their end in similar fashion, the machine was replaced before long, putting Chapman quickly back into the sky.

Still early in its existence, air war was evolving rapidly. One-to-one combat was being replaced by battles of planes in formation, as March describes "…maneuvering as effectively as bodies of cavalry." South of the Argonne Forest in northeastern France, Chapman took to the air as part of a five-plane squadron at 9 a.m. on Friday, May 3rd. After circling near the front lines, off in the distance, the pilots could eventually make out a formation of German planes moving in their direction.

The Allied unit climbed higher, hoping to pounce on the unsuspecting flyers. The plan worked. Startled, the Germans evaded an initial burst of fire, scattered, then reformed, and counterattacked. Planes bearing the markings of each side fired and flew, but to no advantage.

After several minutes, Chapman and an enemy counterpart left their formations and circled. They exchanged blasts with machine guns. Their units and observers on the ground reported that, nearly in unison, each machine burst into flames and lost altitude. Chapman could not have survived the crash which ended his first dogfight. Falling behind German lines, his body was not recovered in the aftermath of the engagement.

News reports of their son's death were delivered to Mr. and Mrs. Chapman at their home shortly after midnight. Although America had formally been at war for more than a year, Lt. Carl Chapman was the first officer from Waterloo to be killed in the fighting. Flags in the community were lowered to half-staff as plans were put in place for remembrance ceremonies. Local newspapers would later note that Chapman held distinction as the first American to be killed in battle while flying a United States Army aircraft.

Precious and heartbreaking all at once, the letter from their son which gave the details his first patrol was delivered to his family a full week after his death. Dated April 22nd, the transatlantic mail had taken eighteen days to cross an ocean and half a continent. On May 29th, one final letter arrived. His last note home was postmarked "May 4," mailed the day after his crash by a member of his unit.

* * *

As Carl Chapman was completing his first term at Amherst, Fred Becker was on the field for another East-West football game in Waterloo. The two-way lineman had become one of the standouts for the orange and black. Playing defense, he was capable of closing the middle of the field and pushing the opposition backwards. On offense, each play started in his hands as the East center.

Late in the 1914 Thanksgiving game, the East High eleven found themselves in a nearly identical position to the one they had faced the year before. West had all the points going into the final quarter, leading 6-0. With a few minutes remaining, East took the football away and drove downfield within two yards of equalizing the score. On third-and-goal, Dick Rath went through the middle of the line, behind Becker, and into the end zone. An extra point later, East was ahead 7-6. As their rivals had done in 1913, East was able to stop the opposition, preserve the lead, and wind down the closing minutes of the game. Becker left the field for the final time as a high school lineman having helped his school even the all-time series against their archrivals at three wins apiece.

Now a senior, Becker graduated with his class in the spring of 1915. Besides playing football, he was a notable basketball player, taking the court as a forward, the same position Carl Chapman had played at West. Becker was also track athlete, made arguments for the East High debate team, and worked to compile the school yearbook. He had been born on November 6, 1895 into a household with a pioneer heritage. His father, John Becker, had come to eastern Iowa in the early 1860's as a child, making at least part of the trip from New York with his family in a covered wagon. Grown up with a family of his own including Fred and two daughters, John Becker had relocated to Waterloo from a farm north of town near 1900.

During the autumn of 1915, Fred Becker moved to Iowa City to continue his education and athletic career at the University of Iowa. He did not play in varsity football games as a freshman while the Hawkeyes struggled through a rough year. After beginning with three wins, Iowa lost the last four games of the season, with three defeats by 16 or more points. Becker, who weighted a little more than 150 pounds, watched from the sidelines and waited his turn while manning the line for the freshman team.

His sophomore season included a place in the varsity starting lineup and a temporary move from center to tackle. Once again, the schedule kicked off with three straight victories, including a 17-7 win versus Grinnell, the small central Iowa college which had been the football program's first opponent ever in 1889. A 67-0 loss to Minnesota in late October – a margin of defeat Iowa has not since suffered during their continuing series with the Gophers – might have seemed like an omen that 1916 was taking a familiar turn for the worse. However, during a November 18th matchup with Iowa State, Becker helped assure the Hawkeyes would avoid their third sub-.500 season of the decade. He blocked two punts, including one which led to a safety, as Iowa won the first of six consecutive meetings against their rivals from Ames, 19-16.

A 34-17 homecoming loss to Nebraska the next week left Iowa with a final mark of 4-3. Becker's play throughout the fall led to recognition for the 20-year-old as one of the top college linemen in the state. The *Chicago Tribune* dubbed him an All-American. With two seasons of eligibility still remaining, Becker was the Hawkeyes' most esteemed player, but he would not take the field the next fall.

In the new year, with the United States' entry into The World War imminent, the All-American left college. Becker enlisted in the Army on March 16th, three weeks before the nation formally entered the conflict. With a partial college education, he was a candidate to become an officer and was sent to Fort Snelling, Minnesota, just outside of St. Paul, for military training. Five months later, he had earned the rank of second lieutenant and was assigned to infantry duty.

In late August, Fred Becker returned to Waterloo and saw his family for the last time before shipping out. His stay at home lasted a little more than a week. On the 27th, relatives and friends accompanied Becker to the Illinois Central station blocks from his home.

"The going away was sad but hopeful," John Becker remembered years later.

Farewells exchanged, the new lieutenant stepped quickly to the train and climbed aboard. By the beginning of October, after passage by ship across the Atlantic, he had joined the American Expeditionary Force in France. Within days, Becker was transferred from the Army to the Marines, who were in need of junior officers. Most of the next several months were spent in training with the men of his unit. Early in 1918, Becker and a small party of troops under his command did engage with a larger force of Germans. The skirmish was a standoff, with the Americans avoiding any casualties.

For Becker and most of the U.S. forces, their time in Europe through nearly the middle of 1918 may have been active with training, but combat was rare. Veteran French and British units still did the bulk of the fighting on the western front as the green Americans were brought up to speed. By May:

> ...the American army numbered more than eight hundred thousand men. They had been getting ready; in camps far behind the lines they had been trained, not only by their own officers, but by some of the greatest experts in the French and British armies. Thousands of officers and men who, but a few months before, had been busily engaged in civilian pursuits, had now learned something of the art of war. They had been supplied with a splendid equipment, with great guns and with all the modern requirements for an up-to-date army.
> (*History of the World War*, Dr. Francis March)

As summer approached, the fresh, well-trained, well-equipped Americans were put into service. The Germans were making a renewed drive toward Paris in hopes of forcing an end to the conflict after nearly four years of war. Moved into forward positions, U.S. forces absorbed the attack north and east of the French capital. They counterattacked and pushed the Germans back.

On June 3rd, Lt. Becker was injured. Pinned down by artillery fire for two hours, an exploding shell fragment was embedded in his right shoulder. Writing a letter home after the incident, he told his family he was "one of a few lucky fellows who escaped in the engagement." Becker was only sidelined for a month, returning to the fight in early July as the enemy continued to fall back before the Allied counter push.

In mid-July, American forces were approaching Chateau-Thierry, about 40 miles away from the outskirts of Paris. Marine units where rushing to the front, one after another, to sustain the offensive, as described by Maj. Robert Denig, who provides an account of his experiences on July 19th:

"The fire got hotter and hotter, men fell, bullets sung, shells whizzed-banged and the dust of battle got thick…A man near me was cut in two. Others when hit would stand, it seemed, an hour then fall in a heap."

Hours earlier and not more than a few miles away, Fred Becker had seen a similar scene in front of him. On July 18th, his men had charged a German machine gun position northwest of Chateau-Thierry, driving away or killing its defenders. Orders came to move forward again. As Becker led his Marines into the open, a bomb exploded in front of him. A piece of shrapnel clipped his neck. From the nature of the wound, the soldiers who later found his body believed he had died instantly.

Lt. Becker, four months shy of his 23rd birthday, was initially buried on the field where he was cut down. An abandoned rifle was spiked into the earth near his shallow grave, made to form a cross when a splintered plank of wood was lashed to its stock. His identity tag was laid over the temporary memorial. When fighting progressed away from the area in succeeding weeks, Becker and the others for who the war had ended on July 18th were moved to a more considered resting place. His family received word of his death on August 7th. The account of his life in the *Times-Tribune* the next day remembered, "He was absolutely fearless on the football field and carried this same spirit into his duties on the battlefield."

November 11, 1918 brought the Armistice, ending hostilities after more than 20 million casualties. Losses to American forces represented roughly 1% of the total. Becker and thousands of others were accorded posthumous American and French honors after their deaths. A more meaningful show of appreciation for their service was an effort to return their remains stateside. In May, 1921, a train carrying Fred Becker's exhumed body in a coffin covered by the American flag pulled into the same station where his family had bidden him farewell in 1917.

Following two days of visitation, overseen at all times by an honor guard of former servicemen, Becker's funeral was held on May 15th at Grace Methodist Episcopal Church. The sanctuary could not hold the thousands who attended. All of the veterans in the Cedar Valley were encouraged to pay their respects. Carloads of Kappa Sigma fraternity brothers – few likely to have known the former Hawkeye – arrived from Iowa City. Pallbearers included East High teammates who had run behind the blocking of the future All-American; Dick Rath, Arthur Simpson, and Gordon Rath now carried their center.

In accordance with his rank as an officer, Becker's remains were drawn by six black horses, first to the church, then to Fairview Cemetery with Waterloo residents looking on as the procession passed. At the graveside, 16 guns volleyed. *Taps* was played. The lieutenant was laid to rest in a ring of veterans surrounding a maple tree, 1st Sgt. Harry Marson to the left and Pvt. Leslie Bruce to the right. The circle would nearly be completed in just a few years by other fallen soldiers returned to Waterloo and former warriors who passed away after coming home to civilian life. Becker's humble limestone marker on a hill in Fairview stands only a few hundred yards from where he played football for East High at Cedar River Park.

* * *

The military aspects of Fred Becker's funeral were managed by the American Legion chapter which bore his name together with Carl Chapman's. Members of Waterloo's Becker-Chapman American Legion Post 138 had been at the train station when the lieutenant's remains arrived. They had helped to plan the service, marched in the funeral procession, and provided the bugler and riflemen at the cemetery.

The broader American Legion organization had been created in France. After the fighting had ceased in 1919, many service members remained in Europe, working on various assignments and awaiting their return home. During this time, the Legion came to life as a fraternal organization. When deployments ended and soldiers traveled back to their communities across the country, they pledged to stay in regular contact with their comrades through this select club, for which membership was only available to participants in The World War. By the end of the 1920's, the organization was composed of 11,000 local posts nationwide, totaling approximately 800,000 Legionnaires.

Post 138 in Waterloo was established in August 1919, sharing Memorial Hall downtown between Fourth and Fifth Streets on the west bank of the Cedar with organizations representing Civil War and Spanish-American War veterans. Five-and-a-half months later, it was renamed to honor Becker and Chapman. Memories of the officers were still vivid in the community. Among the more than 650 local legionnaires who were members of the outfit by the end of 1920, many had known or served with the two fallen lieutenants.

Discharged from their respective branches of the military, former soldiers, sailors, and marines were confronted with challenging realities in the early 1920's. Some still suffered from wounds, physical and psychological, received during a war previously unequaled for its capacity to bring death and terror. The American economy had also slowed. The Rev. Henry Mueller noted the conditions while addressing mourners at Fred Becker's funeral, according to the *Waterloo Courier*, saying, "...that it made his heart ache to see the boys who offered their lives to their country when the call for volunteers came, standing on the streets, now that peace has come, with nothing to do, many of them moneyless and jobless."

The American Legion put substantial effort into mitigating issues like this. At the national level, the organization served as a lobbying group. Their efforts brought federal government attention to veterans' issues, and in 1921 helped establish the agency which later evolved into the Veteran's Administration. The Legion's policies could be dictated from the top down or created from the bottom up, depending on the issue. As might be expected from an association of military men, there was a distinct, regimented structure to the Legion; it was composed of local posts, within regional districts, inside state departments, eventually working up to the national leadership. Meetings and conventions to exchange ideas at all levels were routine. The Becker-Chapman Post hosted the Iowa state convention in September, 1922, with five thousand in attendance. The gathering included notables like National Commander and Iowa native Hanford MacNider and Baseball Commissioner Kenesaw Mountain Landis, a special visitor.

At a grassroots level, Post 138 tried to intervene wherever war veterans were struggling, regardless of whether the former servicemen were members of the organization. Local leaders vouched for comrades who were seeking jobs or bank loans. They negotiated with area hospitals to provide discounted services for sick or injured veterans and their families, sometimes paying the bills from Legion funds when necessary. In the event of troubled times due to physical or financial infirmity, they provided relief by purchasing groceries or other essentials. When a brother-in-arms passed away, the Legion assisted with last military rites.

The Becker-Chapman Post was also broadly involved within Waterloo as a civic organization. Many local legionnaires were in their 20's and 30's, able and enthusiastic family men hoping to make the town they had fought for a better place for their children. In the latter part of the decade, the Waterloo contingent was in regular contention for the MacNider Cup, sponsored by state Legion headquarters and awarded to the outfit with the most notable service efforts. In 1927, Post Commander Arthur Zimmerman – who had formerly been the local chaplain and offered a prayer at Fred Becker's graveside service in 1921 – explained the interest in improving the community, saying, "It is our belief that the ex-serviceman has an obligation to discharge a duty, and an opportunity to perform a service to his community on account of the experience and point of view he gained in the service."

Music was an area of interest. After a couple of failed attempts, the Legion formed a band which debuted on Memorial Day, 1926. The group included 50 players and became a source of special pride, appearing at patriotic events and local festivals. In 1929, the City of Waterloo made it the official community band after residents had voted in favor of a "band tax" to sustain it. The Becker-Chapman Post also founded a 40-man drum and bugle corps in 1927 – capable, according to Commander-elect A.D.

Donnell of "...making martial music such as would inspire a surge of patriotism in the veins of the most ardent pacifist" – and provided annual trophies for the Northeast Iowa High School Music Contest.

With other service organizations, the Legion was particularly interested in helping to establish the first local airport in the Cedar Valley. During 1927, they held special programs and raised funds in preparation for the project east of Waterloo. A little more than a year later in October 1928, the facility was christened "Chapman Field."

For some efforts, the men of the post were particularly well-suited to assist. Coming to Waterloo's rescue in mid-March 1929, 500 to 600 former soldiers were marshaled to spend a weekend fortifying the town with sandbags as the Cedar River flooded. In some cases, Legion members even helped residents escape their homes as the water rose around them, "...demonstrating to the people of Waterloo that they were still its first line of defense," according to the *Waterloo Courier*. The effort, which was credited with minimizing damage to the community, was delivered at some cost; Ben Stickley, a legionnaire answering the call from Parkersburg, became ill as a result of the wet work and never recovered, passing away in the following weeks.

The post funded its relief and service projects in several ways, generating as much as $25,000 in successful years. Annual membership fees in the 1920's ranged from $3.50 to $5 per man or, in some cases, woman. Local veterans who were not active in the organization were encouraged to join with much success. By 1930, the post's rolls included over 950. Each year, the Becker-Chapman Women's Auxiliary – formed in 1921 – sold thousands of red poppies, a tradition which continues even to the present day at posts across the country. During that time, the little paper or cloth flowers carried a well-understood symbolic meaning. The French graves of many soldiers killed in The Great War were covered by poppies, which sprang up in war cemeteries naturally.

Additional fundraising was creatively mixed with sponsorship of various community activities, giving the legion additional exposure as an added benefit. Some projects were more popular than others. Beginning in May 1921, the post organized an annual theatrical production featuring actors from among its membership and the community. That fall, and for many years afterwards, the post managed a much-admired waffle stand during Waterloo's annual Dairy Cattle Congress festivities. When the Legion's national leadership began to advocate consistent rules for proper display and handling of the American flag, Becker-Chapman members instructed local businesses on the procedures, selling them flags and accessories at the same time.

During an era before television, or even radio saturation, sports were popular as ever in local communities. The Legion presented occasional golf tournaments and boxing matches. Then in 1926, the idea was proposed to bring a game to northeast Iowa which most Waterloo residents had never before seen. According to 1930 Post Historian Fred Tesmer, author of the *Becker-Chapman Barrage* newsletter, "…the Post was away on one of the most popular and successful enterprises [it] had ever undertaken."

A CREDITABLE SEXTET

In the fall of 1926, hockey changed forever. The National Hockey League's teams were unchallenged as the best in the world for the first time. The Western Hockey League, based in the Pacific Northwest and Canadian Rockies – the last of several circuits which had shared possession of the Stanley Cup with the NHL – disbanded before the season began. Not only was the NHL now assured that its champion would possess hockey's most important symbol, the league also received a tide of star free agent talent, swept across the continent from the WHL. With all of the sport's top players skating in New York, Toronto, Montreal, Boston, Ottawa, Pittsburgh – and for the first time – Chicago, and Detroit, interest in the game grew substantially.

The evolution of professional hockey at this seminal time had little impact directly on the sport's beginnings in Waterloo. The game was coming to northeast Iowa regardless of its following at higher levels in larger cities to the east. Two years earlier, Roy Malcolm had visited the

National Dairy Cattle Congress in Waterloo, just a few hundred yards from the riverbank opposite Cedar River Park. There, in the spacious Hippodrome exhibition building on the fairgrounds, he could foresee a suitable space for his sport.

Malcolm was born in Winnipeg, Manitoba, on April 1, 1895, the same year as Carl Chapman and Fred Becker. Learning to skate at age five, he played hockey outdoors with two brothers on frozen ponds and backyard rinks throughout long Canadian winters. Malcolm's family moved north and west during his childhood, eventually settling in Red Deer, Alberta. Growing into adolescence, he attended Red Deer High School, then Western Canada College in Calgary. In 1915, while Canada was still part of the British Empire, Malcolm joined the army. As he had in school, the now-20-year-old continued to skate, playing for the 89th Battalion team.

After seeing combat in France, Malcolm returned to the Canadian provinces unscathed. He married his wife, Lois, and they relocated to Iowa in 1922. A year later, they had a son, Alan, in Waterloo. The senior Malcolm worked at Black's department store downtown. As a former soldier during The World War, he was welcomed to the Becker-Chapman Legion. There he was appointed to leadership roles, serving as post chaplain in 1927 and 1928 and as a member of the Becker-Chapman executive council in 1929.

It was December, 1926, when Malcolm presented his idea for hockey at the Hippodrome to Post Commander Arthur Zimmerman and other officials. Together, they hastily decided that an ice rink could be both profitable for the post, while also benefitting the community. Contacting the Dairy Cattle Congress staff, they arranged a lease for winter management of the Hippodrome. Post members volunteered their weekends and busily began to put the pieces in place to give the Cedar Valley its first indoor rink.

While Malcolm was charged with building a hockey team, Ed Brucher was responsible for Becker-Chapman's business operations at the Hippodrome. As post adjutant, nearly every major project the local Legion was involved with was his responsibility to some degree. At age 33 in 1926, Brucher had come to Waterloo before the war from Remsen, Iowa, in the northwestern part of the state. After a three-year course of study at Waterloo Business College, he graduated in 1914 and stayed in the Cedar Valley, working as a bank teller. In 1917, Brucher signed up for the National Guard and went to Europe, serving in an ambulance company. He left active service as a sergeant in 1919, but remained in the military reserve, with an officer's commission beginning in 1924.

Brucher had the big "ice field" at the Hippodrome ready by the end of December. The 200-foot by 100-foot rink opened to skaters for the first time on New Year's Day, 1927. Even without a hockey team, the novelty of indoor ice held promise for a reasonable return on the Legion's investment. Adults came to skate for 25 cents, while kids could zip around the ice for a dime. Under the lustrous glow of lights suspended from the rafters above, ladies in long dresses and men in suit coats and derby caps could circle the rink after work and the winter sunset. Hippodrome guests enjoyed music while skating, thanks to a radio on loan from a local furniture store hoping to promote the still-new technological innovation and expand the market for its devices.

"This is the biggest indoor ice rink in the middlewest.

There is ample room for 500 skaters at one time," Brucher boasted in mid-January. Through that point, attendance was averaging 200 people per day, with larger crowds on weekends.

Recreational hockey was being played at the Hippodrome each evening from 7 to 8 p.m. A notice to anyone interested in learning the sport appeared in the January 15th edition of the *Waterloo Courier*. Within a week, enough players had answered the call to hold shinny games. It was hoped that the Old Pals team, sponsored by the Des Moines Athletic Club, might be able to come to Waterloo for a game at the end of the month.

Like Malcolm, others who had relocated to the Cedar Valley from hockey communities to the north or east joined the Waterloo team as it formed. Fred "Hans" Wagner was another Legion member with experience on ice. Goalie George Watson was originally from upstate New York. Forward L.H. Beaton was said to have had some success playing minor professional hockey in Saskatchewan. Eventually, he coaxed his former teammate, Bill Hunter, to play in Waterloo while going to college in Des Moines. With Hunter came Joe Shelledy, who had a reputation as a marathon speed skater. C.C. Gorrell, an Ottawa native, migrated south after minding the net for several seasons in the central Canadian provinces.

The game versus the Old Pals was finally set for Saturday, February 5th. There was enough anticipation for the matchup that several Legion players trekked to Des Moines to scout their opponent on the Sunday before the contest. The Old Pals were reportedly undefeated in at least a half dozen games against other central Iowa teams that winter. When added to their success from previous seasons, they were considered the informal hockey state champions in the same way a boxer might be given a championship title after defeating all of the notable contenders in his weight class.

Unfortunately for players and curious sports fans alike, the weather turned unseasonably warm during the first week of February. The Hippodrome was shut up tight the entire week prior to the scheduled encounter, but with no artificial cooling system in the building, organizers had to hope colder temperatures would come along to save the contest. Brucher remained positive, telling reporters that the game "...will be played Saturday night unless another tornado hits the Cattle Congress – and this is a little early for tornados."

Notwithstanding the adjutant's forecast, a heavy rain fell on the eve of the matchup. It was not as powerful as the September 1925 windstorm Brucher had referenced. That weather event had included the destruction of three 10,000-square foot fairgrounds barns when their roofs were blown in, costing an estimated $15,000 to repair. However the rains on February 4th made hockey against the Old Pals impossible the next day. The rink had been flooded, leaving the ice in sorry condition.

The game was pushed back a week to February 12th, and the weather cooperated. Cold air more typical of early February returned, giving the Legion players their first opportunity to resume practice on the Tuesday before the matchup. They had been off the ice for ten days. Tickets were put on sale at the Becker-Chapman office and friendly business locations in downtown Waterloo. Adults could get in for 50 cents and kids for 25, prices comparable to those of the Waterloo Hawks baseball team, which at that time spent summers playing in the Mississippi Valley League in front of large crowds.

Following a last practice on February 10th, *Courier* sportswriters were confident enough to predict, "Waterloo's hockey team will stack up creditably against any sextet in the middlewest."

By late Saturday evening, 1,500 people had found their way to the Hippodrome for the inaugural hockey game in Waterloo. In addition to the featured event, the Legion Band was on hand to provide music. Shelledy and figure skater Edith Gray each gave a skating performance for the crowd. When the puck dropped, the pace of play amazed those who had gathered. The *Courier* recounted, "...you can't convince a single soul of...[those] who witnessed the hockey match in the Dairy Cattle Congress Hippodrome Saturday evening that hockey isn't the fastest game..." The local side took the lead in the first period when Hunter weaved around traffic to fire a shot into the cage. A pair of quick goals by Des Moines then allowed the visitors to seesaw in front. After the score was retied briefly, the Old Pals carried a 3-2 edge to intermission.

In the second, Waterloo pulled ahead for good. In fact, offense picked up considerably for both sides over the remaining 40 minutes, and at the end of regulation, the Legion club owned a 13-8 victory. It was a physical game; playing defense Malcolm had been knocked around and was suffering from bruised ribs when it was over. The crowd left the rink in a celebratory mood; after just one game, their team could style itself as the champion of Iowa hockey after beating the previous titleholder.

* * *

On the ice in 1927, a puck put past the goalie and into the

mesh behind counted as a goal. The team with the most goals won. Other resemblances to the modern sport were limited. Even the material which composed that net behind the goaltender were different; pliable wire caught flying pucks, before being replaced with twine in later years.

During play, carrying the puck was much more important than passing. Forward passes were not legal outside the defensive zone. At center ice and in offensive territory, players were only allowed to connect laterally across the rink or backwards, as forward passing was considered offside. There was an exception only if an opponent touched the puck before it was received. Not surprisingly, icing rules would not be introduced for another decade as there was little excuse to feed the puck far ahead.

Six players still took the ice at full strength, but only a couple of substitutes waited on the bench to relieve them. Goalies didn't wear masks; forwards and defensemen went without helmets, although some wore stocking caps, which at least protected a player from the cold, if not the puck or an opponent. They carried straight-bladed sticks with just a few widths of tape at the tip and wore warm, thick sweaters. Some skaters would play the entire 60 minute contest. At a minimum, a shift might last three minutes. When a change was made, the player coming onto the rink not only replaced his counterpart, but also had to check-in quickly with the referee during the process.

Defenders inside their own blue line were the only ones allowed to deliver body checks. Kicking the puck in the offensive zone was illegal but allowed in defensive and neutral areas. Anyone skating around the rink who carried his stick above shoulder level could be called for a penalty. While games were rougher, fewer penalties were actually called. However, when someone did land in the penalty box, he stayed for a full two minutes, regardless of how many goals were scored during the resulting shorthanded situation.

While several of the details might have been different in that era, the *Courier* editorialized that the sport caught on due to its freeform nature: "If any one thing makes hockey popular, it is the decided lack of rules...the absence of rules makes hockey fast. When a substitute or spare enters the game, the contest is not stopped while he reports to the official...Hockey is better off for its lack of playing rules."

It was certainly much different than the high school or college basketball games of the time, which might very well end with an exciting final score like 13-12.

Waterloo's early hockey games were overseen on ice by a single referee. Since the sport was a new attraction in the community, natives with adequate skating ability and knowledge of the rules were not easy to find for the job. As hockey became established, former opponents were hired to call penalties when their teams were not playing against Waterloo or elsewhere. If that was not an option, a prospective or former Legion player not currently skating for the club might be handed the assignment. This created an obvious conflict of interest, pointed out explicitly on at least one occasion when Hans Wagner was the referee during a 1930 contest. However, no such concerns were noted in relation to Waterloo's second matchup in February, 1927. While the game official had previously been a Cedar Valley resident, both sides were apparently satisfied with the impartiality of Father A.L. McGreavy – also a former athletic coach at St. Mary's College in Winona, Minnesota – when he returned for a visit from his St. Rose parish in Lewiston, Minnesota.

The opponent for Game Two was a collection of players from north of Sioux City in the communities around Le Mars. The squad was led by Lee Herron, a noted amateur golfer. Besides his accomplishments on the links, Herron had sharpened his hockey skills while attending the University of Minnesota. Le Mars' goalie Charles von Berg was also locally notable, having lived in Waterloo briefly as a child. That was decades before he eventually picked up hockey in western Iowa; von Berg was over 60 years old when he appeared in net at the Hippodrome for the Le Mars Independents.

One week after opening their impromptu schedule with a win, the Legion six were back on ice in front of a crowd similar in size to the one they had impressed while hosting the Old Pals. George Watson replaced Gorrell in goal. A Canadian winger named Pat Murphy filled in for the absent Shelledy. Although still sore, Roy Malcolm was in the starting lineup, however it was his big defense partner, Wagner, who gave the home team an early jolt.

In addition to patrolling the ice with Malcolm during the early games staged by the Becker-Chapman Post, Wagner was also given equal regard with his defensemate for bringing the sport to the community. According to the *Courier* as it recapped the first year of Waterloo hockey, "These two men, both members of the American Legion under whose colors the local team plays, prevailed on the Legion to sponsor a team…and immediately the game took such a foothold that the city would be lost without its regular hockey matches now."

Wagner was said to have skated with amateur teams in Ontario. From there, he found his way to Chicago and played semiprofessionally for a time. Landing in Waterloo, he took a job, like Malcolm, at Black's department store. Serving as a defenseman at the rink, Wagner was rugged, unapologetically giving opponents a whack when they came to the front of the net. Versatile, he was occasionally used as a forward and even considered as a goaltender early in the 1927/28 season before the Legion found a more natural player for the position. Slowed by nagging leg injuries in 1928 and gaining significant weight during the offseason, Wagner left the team but could often be found at the rink when not enjoying his other favorite pastime, hunting.

Just 1:10 into the action against Le Mars, Wagner notched an early goal. He added to the margin eleven minutes later, and the score held at 2-0 through 20 minutes. The visitors answered with two goals of their own during the second period, but Malcolm helped Waterloo recover the advantage at the ten minute mark, then again at 15:45 after the Independents had rebounded to make it 3-3 momentarily.

Early in the third, the Waterloo captain completed a hat trick, allowing the Legion to reestablish a two-goal lead. It stood for ten minutes before a tally by Herron, then another for Le Mars in short order – the second of the night by Charley Yount – erased the advantage completely. Despite five goals allowed, von Berg had delivered a number of quality stops for the visitors among his 16 saves and was close to delivering the contest to the end of regulation squared at 5-5. Then Malcolm found the puck on the opposite side of the rink, "…and weaving, feigning, dodging, and dribbling, he advanced it to the Le Mars goal, where after a furious scrimmage, he shot it against the wire barrier for what proved to be the winning marker."

The thrilling 6-5 victory behind four goals from the founding father of Waterloo hockey stirred anticipation for more of the sport. For Malcolm, it was the first of many performances which would make him a local sporting celebrity. Away from hockey, the modest-looking gentleman in his early 30's with a high forehead and wire-rimmed glasses may not have given the impression of a fierce athletic competitor. However, over four seasons at the Hippodrome, Malcolm would only rarely miss his shift, having a hand in all of the success Waterloo enjoyed at the rink.

* * *

In early 1927, excitement for hockey had spread to Texas. The biggest cities in that state had built ice rinks and filled them with teams of players imported from the north. Promoters overcame the difficulties caused by the natural southern climate with cooling and ice-making systems similar to those used in the major hockey venues of the time, ensuring a playable surface despite the weather.

Waterloo fans were more and less fortunate than their Lone Star state counterparts all at once. Funds were not available to build a modern 1920's hockey rink in a community where few had ever seen a game prior to the Legion's endeavor. As a non-profit organization, the Legion itself was certainly in no position to take on such a project. However, the Cedar Valley did have the Dairy Cattle Congress facilities, which had been hosting large crowds during autumn agricultural events for over a decade. Northeast Iowa also had geography. Players from communities farther to the north could reach Waterloo without too much difficulty whether they were coming to skate for or against the local club. It was also typically cold enough during the winter months to maintain a rink with only natural efforts.

Keeping the Hippodrome ice playable was not quite as simple as opening the arena doors and letting the cold air blow in. When frigid weather settled on the area, the building's cement floor was flooded. After the ice had formed in the unheated enclosure, the process might be repeated multiple times. If temperatures rose for a prolonged stretch, the initial effort could be entirely wiped out. After a base layer was successfully put down, a finer coating of water would be sprayed onto the rink to provide a truer surface. On some occasions, the ice at the Dairy Cattle Congress grounds was layered as much as a foot thick. By comparison, other rinks circulating chilled antifreeze through pipes embedded in their concrete floors have ice measuring just an inch deep. This prevents melting and pooling close to the surface. In the Hippodrome, making the ice as thick as possible was a necessity; an extended period of warm weather had the potential to postpone skating activities indefinitely if all of the ice melted.

In the event of a heat wave, Legion officials might close the building, as they did prior to the original date set for the Old Pals game. More creatively, in early March 1927, they doused the roof of the facility with icy water in order to keep it as cool as possible. During subsequent seasons, several varieties of ice scrapers were employed to shave the rink before games. As long as base had been built to an adequate thickness, the softer top layer could be removed when conditions were moderate, providing the players a much smoother surface.

Becker-Chapman leaders did consider retrofitting the building to have more reliable ice after observing the popularity of hockey and skating programs. The project would have cost at least $10,000, a figure which no one ever made a concerted effort to raise. In spite of the Hippodrome's limitations, in late 1927 the community was still reportedly under consideration to become the home of the Iowa State Skating Association's headquarters. The body had chapters across the northern part of the state. Working under the overarching governance of the Amateur Athletic Union and International Skating Union, the state-level body hoped to provide the best local ice athletes an opportunity to qualify for national and international events.

For the Legion hockey team, two weeks passed while they waited for their next game after the Le Mars win. Part of the delay was due to an Ice Derby scheduled at the rink for community youth. However that event was postponed by balmy weather, which limited hockey playing as well. While local skaters were idle, the opponent for the final contest of the season changed. After announcing that the game would be against the Chicago Athletic Association, team officials backtracked a few days later, naming the St. Paul Hook 'em Cows as the visiting side.

The Cows had been an anticipated opponent in early February. When the season's initial hockey game versus Des Moines was delayed a week, St. Paul had been bumped from the schedule. The club's name was representative of the connections its players had to the stockyards in South St. Paul. They were reportedly the best team in the Southern Minnesota Hockey Association, and one of the top amateur teams in the Twin Cities. During the first seasons of Waterloo hockey, games with the Cows would represent a significant measuring stick for the quality of the Legion squad.

Anticipating that St. Paul would be a stronger opponent

than anything they had seen, Malcolm spent the week prior to the game making preparations to bulk up his roster with ringers. He brought in Charley Yount, originally from Saskatchewan, who had played well against the Legion for Le Mars. Also added were a goaltender named Bishop, plus forwards Smith and Goodwill (or possibly "Goodwillie"). Neither the original teams these players skated for, nor even their first names, were recorded in the records which remain from the game. Malcolm and Wagner were the only starters from Waterloo's first two contests who remained in the lineup, opening the affair at defense when the Hook 'em Cows visited on March 5th.

During the initial period, St. Paul carried the play, controlling the puck and limiting the Legion side to just three shots on goal. Scoring eight minutes into the game, then again with 30 seconds left before intermission, the Cows owned a 2-0 lead after one frame. Waterloo cut the margin in half when Smith's shot hit the back of the cage halfway through the second. The Legion did not have enough time to tally an equalizer however, before Earle Willey and Roy Westphalinger each scored goals just a minute apart. In the third period, Yount notched a pair of markers, but St. Paul answered within seconds each time, as Westphalinger recorded his second of the game midway through the period and Willey celebrating the same accomplishment with less than a minute remaining.

The final score was 6-3 in front of a record crowd of approximately 3,000 fans. The Cows outshot the local club 25-12, with the entire contest played at even strength. St. Paul impressed the reporter on hand to take down the details for the *Courier*, who noted, "…the superior team play of St. Paul counted in the end. The winners were adept at passing the puck back and forth and between, and rarely did a skater lose the puck for lack of a mate to shoot it to."

Many of the players whom the Cows brought to the Cedar Valley would become increasingly familiar to local hockey fans over time. Willey, who also contributed an assist in addition to his two goals, jumped to the Legion team the following winter. Defenseman Gordon Brown came along a few years later. Westphalinger was on the ice for several of the biggest matchups in Legion hockey history, making the trip from the Twin Cities to serve as referee.

Becker-Chapman members rightfully considered their first season at the rink a success. Monetarily, hockey tickets and skating admissions had generated a profit of nearly $400 after all of the expenses were deducted. The effort had also captured the attention and acclaim of many in the community. Between the boards, the team's 2-1 record was very respectable, especially when considering the limited experience of the club and that few of the players had ever previously skated together. During the spring and summer, the post's attention was turned to a variety of other projects. However, there was no doubt regarding the return of hockey and Hippodrome ice once the days on the calendar began to dwindle. Waterloo had become a hockey town.

BIGGER AND BETTER

Throughout 1927, Waterloo residents unfolded their newspapers to read about Charles Lindbergh becoming an American hero after flying solo across the Atlantic Ocean. They followed the scandalous accounts of actor Charlie Chaplin's divorce proceedings with syndicated wire reports from the courtroom. The sports section detailed Babe Ruth's most notable season as he became the first slugger in major league baseball to hit 60 home runs in one summer. By mid-October, long before the weather or the Hippodrome were ready, Legion hockey was already being discussed in print and anticipation for a new season was building.

A month later, work was underway to prepare the arena floor. Ice would be available considerably ahead of the 1926/27 schedule. Post officials targeted December 1st as the date when skating would begin. Although that projection proved to be overly optimistic, when the rink did open on Sunday, the 11th, 500 to 600 enthusiasts were on hand with their skates. The first hockey contest of the new season was arranged for the following Saturday.

The Legion Team

The promise of a heavy schedule, strong attendance, a share of the money from gate receipts, and fulltime jobs during the week, meant hockey players began to arrive in Waterloo while the ice was still being layered. The transplanted residents would form a squad which, unlike the previous season's club, would largely remain together with few changes for the entire winter. Defenseman Bob Collette was dubbed the Legion team's captain. He came to the Cedar Valley in early December with forward Louis Webber, a fellow White Bear Lake, Minnesota, native. Charley Yount returned to join the team as a regular after appearing for Waterloo against the Hook 'em Cows. Clarence Keyes and Paul Berkey, Yount's teammates previously in Drinkwater, Saskatchewan, also found their way to the Dairy Cattle Congress grounds.

The most exciting addition for fans who had come to the rink during the previous season was forward Earle Willey. The Twin Cities native had delivered an impressive performance against Waterloo when the Cows had upended the Legion in March. Another aspect of Willey's immediate popularity was the claim by the *Courier* that he had been part of the 1924 U.S. Olympic delegation. That National Team had earned a silver medal during the games in France, averaging 18 goals per matchup against outclassed European opponents, before eventually falling to Canada. However, modern records fail to confirm that Willey was part of the American squad, suggesting instead that his exploits may have been confused with those of his former St. Paul Saints teammate, Taffy Able, a '24 Olympic hockey star who went on to play in the NHL for New York and Chicago, winning the Stanley Cup twice.

Although Willey may not have actually played in the

Olympics, he did have a great deal of experience. The dark-haired skater had joined the Cows only shortly before they traveled to Waterloo, spending most of the 1926/27 season in Michigan's Upper Peninsula Hockey League with the Ironwood Rangers. Willey had also been in northern Michigan the winter prior to that as a member of the Sault Ste. Marie Greyhounds. The *Courier* noted his skills, saying, "...his all-around skating was a treat for sore eyes. He handles the stick deftly and he is as elusive as a shadow when dribbling the puck up ice." Like many of his teammates, Willey took up residence at the Brockwell Arms Apartments on Jefferson Street in downtown Waterloo.

Roy Malcolm and Fred Wagner were the only carryovers from the beginning of the previous season. With the addition of substantial talent, Malcolm intended to take a smaller role on the ice, serving as a playing manager: making scheduling arrangements with opposing teams, coaching, and skating in reserve off the bench on game day. Meanwhile, Wagner was assigned a goalie's stick and pads, charged with manning that position throughout early December workouts. It looked likely that he would start in net during the opening game until newcomer Bill Vaughan arrived to take the position on December 16th, one day before the matchup.

For the second consecutive year, the Becker-Chapman Post began hockey season with a game against the Des Moines Old Pals. During their first visit to the Hippodrome, the Old Pals had owned a lead after 20 minutes, but in the rematch, they never got started. Willey scored twice in the first period, with Keyes striking in between for a 3-0 margin at intermission. The Legion players added two more goals in the second period, then broke the contest open with eight in the third. The 13-0 victory required just four saves by Vaughan. Willey and Keyes each were credited with five goals. Malcolm's confident pregame comments claiming, "There is no comparison between this year's six and last year's and fans who witness the match Saturday are bound to be agreeably surprised," captured the improvement entirely.

The Waterloo, Cedar Falls, and Northern Railroad had carried carloads of passengers to the game on streetcars. An even larger crowd was expected for the next matchup, just over a week later on the day after Christmas. The opponent was slated to be a team from Akron, Iowa, spiked with several of the skaters from the Le Mars squad which had given the Legion a nail-biting game the previous February. After a light Christmas Day practice, everyone in a Legion sweater was ready to play.

Unfortunately, their opponents were not as well prepared. Only four Akron players made it to the rink in time for the 3:30 opening faceoff. They had taken a train, while their teammates elected to hold onto the money sent for railway tickets and instead make the nearly 250 mile trip driving through small towns and opens spaces on Grant Highway, which weaved from one end of the state to the other between Dubuque and Sioux City. At 4 PM, they had still not arrived, and the game began without them. Berkey and Brock Richardson, a recent arrival to Waterloo who hoped for a place on the team, filled out the visiting lineup. Malcolm joined in too, playing off the bench for Akron and recording the visitors' only first period goal *against* Waterloo. The score stood at 6-1 when the Akron reinforcements arrived to play the second.

Keys and Willey starred in another victory for the locals. The center from the rural plains near Moose Jaw,

Saskatchewan, had a hat trick within the first 17 minutes, then added another goal in the second period. Playing at left wing, Willey scored three times. On this occasion, Vaughn was called on for 18 saves as the Legion outshot Akron 43-20. More than 3,500 fans cheered the 10-2 win.

Days later, as the *Courier* looked back on 1927 in its New Year's Eve edition, the paper editorialized, "The American Legion is to be complimented for its initiative in introducing this great winter sport. As a community achievement it ranks at the top of the list."

Waterloo's hockey team was only beginning to build *its* list of achievements.

* * *

As the calendar turned to 1928, and after two games which had been runaway victories, Waterloo hockey fans anticipated a rematch against the only opponent to ever defeat the local team. On the afternoon of Monday, January 2nd, the Becker-Chapman Legion hoped a big crowd celebrating a long holiday weekend would help push the club past the Hook 'em Cows. Optimistic estimates for as many as 5,000 spectators were mentioned. Unfortunately, extreme temperatures which barely crept to zero limited attendance to around 2,000.

The Becker-Chapman squad leapt ahead just over two minutes into the game thanks to a goal from Louis Webber. Clarence Keyes added another at 6:10, then scored again at 18:14, just the beginning of his big day. The centerman was nearly unstoppable, adding three more in the second period, then two in the third for a grand total of seven goals in the Legion's 10-5 victory. Former St. Paul forward Earle Willey contributed a tally for Waterloo, and goalie Bill Vaughan –

who had also skated with the Cows at one time during his hockey travels – delivered a solid effort, making 26 saves and holding the visitors to just two goals in the first 55 minutes before they made the score a little more balanced in the closing shifts. The matchup was as physical as it was lopsided, and the "barked shins and bruised knees and elbows" mentioned in the *Courier*'s write-up would nag at several of the participants for weeks to come.

Although the first game in the Cedar Valley's hockey history had been postponed by unseasonably warm weather eleven months earlier, local promoters of the sport discovered that bitter cold temperatures were not any better for business. Determined spectators may have been heartened by an encouraging preview story in the newspaper which advised "...the rink is indoors, the cold will not be keenly felt, tho fans are urged to bring along blankets to keep legs and feet from becoming chilled." Less hearty fans just decided to stay home. Although the hippodrome walls may have slowed the wind and retained some of the warmth generated by those at the rink, with no artificial temperature controls, the air inside the building was typically only around 20 degrees warmer than the conditions outside on a day like January 2nd.

Those who were intent to see the Legion team play found creative ways to battle the frigid temperatures during trips to the Hippodrome. On the advice of players used to colder northern climates, some massaged distilled plant oils into their feet before putting on their socks and shoes. Others watched the action while perching their boots on bricks which had been warmed on a stove and toted from home. Becker-Chapman officials understood quickly how weather could affect their project. For big games, they sought help from military forecasters at Great Lakes Naval Station north of Chicago to decide how to proceed before bringing an opponent into town.

Besides weather reports, the Chicago area would also regularly supply opposing hockey teams from the city's Senior Amateur Hockey League, beginning with the skaters from the Chicago Athletic Association on the first Friday of January, 1928. The club had begun fielding a hockey team in 1926 and skated regularly on the same Chicago Coliseum ice which had become home to the NHL's Chicago Black Hawks that winter. The Athletic Association embraced the sport and hoped to expand its local popularity, with officials telling the *Chicago Daily Tribune* that, "There ought to be as many hockey rinks as baseball diamonds in the city."

Formed nearly 40 years earlier, CAA was a fraternal meeting place for the city's athletically-minded business professionals. Its teams wore a distinctive logo on their uniforms, a "C" with a ring around it – both red – leading to the club's nickname, "The Cherry Circle." From its Michigan Avenue headquarters, the organization fielded teams in a variety of sports and faced opponents on all manner of athletic grounds throughout the Midwest. Less than two months after sending their hockey squad to Waterloo, for example, the Athletic Association track and field team was in Iowa City running against the Hawkeyes.

On the ice, CAA had a strong squad, earning the title of top senior team in Chicago the previous winter. They had also claimed a cup from a regional tournament in St. Louis in 1927, part of an impressive collection of hardware. According to the *Waterloo Courier*, U.S. Olympic officials had hoped CAA would travel to Switzerland as the nation's entry for the 1928 Winter Games. However, the plan was scrapped because the Athletic Association roster included too many Canadians.

Among the imported players were John Carrick and Freddie Robertson, who had played college hockey in Ontario and Manitoba respectively. Defenseman Charlie Carson was a former junior player from Toronto. Closer to Chicago, CAA also enjoyed connections to the University of Notre Dame. Team manager Tom Shaughnessy had played for the fledgling Irish hockey program while obtaining his degree in the early 1910's. More than a decade later, he was lawyer who coached at the Athletic Association in his spare time. After the 1928/29 season, Shaughnessy would go directly from CAA to become head coach of the Chicago Black Hawks, a position which changed hands almost annually – and often more than once per winter – during the franchise's early years. Although he resigned unexpectedly in early 1930 after a spat with team owners, his career results in the league included ten wins, eight losses, and three ties, leaving his record above .500. The Black Hawks held second place in the NHL's American Division when Shaughnessy announced that he was quitting. Shaughnessy also holds the distinction of coaching the Hawks during their first game in the newly-constructed Chicago Stadium, a 3-1 victory versus the Pittsburgh Pirates, on December 16, 1929.

An Illinois Central locomotive pulled Shaughnessy and his Athletic Association boys to Waterloo on the morning of their first meeting with Becker-Chapman. Their arrival time allowed for a practice at the Hippodrome. The evening paper glowed about the CAA players' reaction to the rink, saying "They expressed astonishment that a city of the size of Waterloo should have such a magnificent rink, and their enthusiasm was keen."

With more comfortable weather than the bitter conditions of earlier in the week and the Legion band on hand, a crowd estimated at 3,500 made their way to the Cattle Congress grounds. The puck dropped around 8:15, and nearly halfway through the first period, the locals pulled ahead as Willey scored off of a feed from Keyes. However, before intermission, Waterloo's outlook took a turn for the worse as Willey injured his back. Reserve Brock Richardson took advantage of additional ice time, making the score 2-0 in the second. Then less than two minutes into the final frame, Keyes put in a shot from a sharp angle. Chicago was held without a goal until 17:12 when Carson scored from close range. During the 3-1 victory, the Legion had outscored and out-chanced (27-20) a club which might have gone to the Olympics. Waterloo now owned an undefeated 4-0 record to open the 1927/28 season.

* * *

In the week following Waterloo's win against the Chicago Athletic Association, the Legion's Roy Malcolm and Ed Brucher visited the local Lions Club. Over lunch in Black's Tea Room downtown, they highlighted the thrilling aspects of hockey. Together, the team manager and post adjutant encouraged those who hadn't already been to the Hippodrome to visit the rink. Undoubtedly, they believed that Lions Club members and anyone else who gave the sport a try would enjoy the action.

Becker-Chapman efforts promoting hockey to a largely unfamiliar audience had the enthusiastic support of the *Waterloo Courier*. It's unclear whether the paper's sportswriters were strongly influenced by the information provided by Malcolm and the Legion, or whether they were simply excited to have another winter activity in the community. Game accounts consistently rang with exuberant hyperbole, exemplified by a write-up in early February, which pronounced, "...if winter strings along into August, it is doubtful another such epic struggle will be seen." Headlines, especially in advance of a weekend contest, exhorted readers that seemingly every opponent would be a spectacular challenge for the locals, and that during the next game the "Legion Hockey Team Expects Stiffest Match of the Season Friday" (January 30, 1928).

Due to the way Waterloo's games were scheduled, having a hockey story printed within the three-cent, six-day-a-week paper was essential for reaching both potentially unfamiliar spectators and regular fans in an era before any form of electronic communication – including radio – was universal in Cedar Valley homes. Game dates or opponents were sometimes unknown until just a few days before the teams met. There were no pocket schedules or posters featuring the entire hockey calendar available for distribution at beginning of the season. When known a week in advance, information about the date, time, and opponent for the Becker-Chapman squad's next game was important enough to regularly lead a postgame story, ahead of results and details describing the action of the night before. Obligingly, the *Courier* editors also ran a brief hockey story about the next tilt nearly every weekday, even when there was little or no new information to report since the previous edition.

Not all of the printed plugs for hockey were free. The Legion regularly purchased newspaper ads to get the word out about what would happen next on the Cattle Congress grounds, reminding readers that admission was just 50 cents. Friendly businesses, many owned or managed by Legion members, also devoted some of their promotional space to the upcoming game. Some made special offers, including free hockey tickets as an incentive to purchase a new radio or other substantial item. By the 1928/29 season, some messages took up entire newspaper pages with as many as 16 different companies – including major businesses like John Deere, Rath Packing, and Iowa Public Service – contributing to the effort. A big ad, like the one in the sports section on January 31, 1929, could contain paragraphs of persuasion:

> The Waterloo American Legion is providing the FASTEST AND MOST DARING GAME OF THEM ALL. It has taken a lot of work on the part of the Legion boys to give to Waterloo sport-loving fans a game they should support and are bound to enjoy if they have any red blood in them. Hockey is not a ping pong contest and the best 'Bridge hound' in the country would fall far short of specifications. It is a regular 'he' game and you don't have to guess whether the boys are trying to win or are laying down. The evidence is out there on the ice. The American Legion has a bunch of fighters on its team and they are never thru fighting until the final whistle.
>
> There are no complicated rules in the game of Hockey. You do not have to be a student of the game to understand and enjoy it. The first-nighters get a big kick out of it.
>
> You baseball, football, basketball and fight fans who want action can get a thrill a second if you are looking for speed. It's at the Hockey Games! Let's get behind the Legion and its Hockey team and go to the game tomorrow night...

Promotional efforts ahead of the team's fifth 1927/28 game helped draw 2,000 people to the rink to see the Legion host the South St. Paul Cowboys, essentially a rebranded version of the Hook 'em Cows, who had visited not quite two weeks earlier. Increasingly warm weather after the below-zero start to January made for bad ice. However, it didn't slow Earle Willey, who had recovered from the knocks he had suffered versus the Chicago Athletic Association. With a close, physical game underway early in the third period, Willey scored twice in less than two minutes "...in almost identical fashion, back-checking to grab the puck in mud ice and racing down the field past the lone defenseman to shoot it under [Arnie] Mentes and into the netting." The goals helped secure a 4-0 decision, supporting a 22-save shutout by Bill Vaughan.

A week later on January 20th, with colder weather and better ice, four goals were again enough to keep the Legion undefeated. This time the opponent was Chicago's Lake Shore Athletic Club. Three of Waterloo's scores came in the final three minutes of the second period – two from Clarence Keyes – stretching the lead to 4-0 at the second intermission. Lake Shore's Connie Joseph scored twice in the third period as the Becker-Chapman squad coasted to a 4-2 decision. There were 1,800 in the stands.

Success, coupled with a slight dip in attendance and added expenses from four consecutive opponents imported across state lines, led the seven-member Legion hockey committee to boost ticket prices. It was announced that henceforth, admission would be 75 cents, with box seats going to a full dollar. For the moment, hockey's popularity in Waterloo was great enough for the increase to be absorbed. The largest crowds that the team would ever host made their way to the rink in the succeeding months for the biggest games the club would ever play.

* * *

When the Hippodrome home team took the ice to begin the 1927/28 season, they wore no helmets, carried their sticks in leather gloves reaching a third of the way to the elbow, and dressed in dark jerseys and socks, with white hockey pants. The players skated with considerably less padding than what would become standard in later generations, so their sweaters were tight-fitting, intended as much as anything to block the cold. Each sleeve was marked with a half dozen horizontal white pinstripes. The circular white logo on the chest contained a pair of diagonally crossed hockey sticks, with a letter "W" above the intersection, then "A" and "L" to a viewer's left and right respectively, standing for "Waterloo American Legion." White wings came off each side of the circle, and the team was occasionally referred to as the "Hawks," the same nickname given to Waterloo's baseball team.

On January 26th, the squad wore brand new uniforms. The patriotic red and white color scheme had the Legion emblem on the chest just below the word "Waterloo". The patriotic colors would have been almost as well-suited to their opponents, a group of soldiers attached to the Third Infantry from Fort Snelling in Minnesota. The same base where Fred Becker had trained after enlisting in 1917 was providing the opposition for the Becker-Chapman Post hockey team not quite a decade after Becker's death in France.

Waterloo was without Fred Wagner for the Thursday night contest. The defenseman had been bothered for several days by a charley horse. Roy Malcolm, who had spent much of the season in a reserve role, stepped into the starting lineup to take his place for the customary 8:15 opening faceoff as fans came to the rink on a crisp, chilly evening.

Brock Richardson opened the scoring during the closing minutes of the first period. Bob Collette set up his first goal, then less than a minute later, Richardson struck again, unassisted. By scoring in rapid succession, the Legion added to the lead shortly after intermission; Earle Willey and Louis Webber each tucked in chances, separated by 39 seconds. However, the Fort Snelling unit was nearly able to erase the 4-0 deficit before the next break, scoring three goals in the last ten minutes of the period, two by Sgt. Steve Mickey. Unfortunately for the soldiers, Waterloo's goals continued to come in pairs. Clarence Keyes nudged the home side ahead by two with just over 15 minutes to play in regulation. On the ensuing faceoff, Willey snagged the puck and zipped into the offensive zone to flip in another chance. Fort Snelling managed just one additional point in the 6-4 decision.

When the Legion tested their still-perfect record just over a week later, they faced an opponent likely to have been as well-equipped as any to ever visit the Cattle Congress in that era. The American House Furnishings squad had connections to a Minnesota sporting goods company. Team manager R.L. Einck was also one of principal partners in the business. Like Waterloo, American House Furnishings had defeated both the Hook 'em Cows and the troops from Fort Snelling.

Twenty-five hundred spectators watched the matchup, which was fast-paced despite reportedly soft ice. The Legion took an early lead 2:10 into the action when Webber stole a puck to set up a successful chance for Keyes, but Waterloo had trouble pulling away. Keyes assisted on a

Willey goal before the first intermission, however the lead was cut in half by the mid-second period. Richardson nudged the home side back ahead by two heading to the third. Tension built with just over eight minutes remaining in regulation when a visiting winger named Warburton cut the lead back to one. From there, American House Furnishings, "...bombarded the Waterloo net unceasingly," according to Julius Johnson's account in the *Courier*. Goalie Bill Vaughan was equal to the rest of the shots which came his way, and Waterloo held on for their closest victory of the winter up to that point, 3-2.

Later in the weekend, the Waterloo Hockey Club made a rare trip out of town. The team traveled to north central Iowa to give an exhibition of the sport at Clear Lake, and an estimated crowd of 3,000 bundled up to watch the outdoor show on a cold, windy Sunday. It was hoped that the performance might spur Mason City sports fans to organize a team of their own for the following season.

Vaughan did not travel with the Legion club. Instead, he arrived separately in Clear Lake after having joined his former St. Paul teammates for a Saturday fill-in appearance in Winona, Minnesota. Described as "husky," the 20-year-old Vaughan had come to Waterloo after opening the 1927/28 season in Dallas, leading sportswriters to note, "He has played the game from Canada to the Gulf and his equal has not been seen on the local ice during the two years hockey has thrived here." By early February, Vaughan's play in Waterloo had already earned him an invitation to try out for the professional Kansas City Pla-Mors of the American Hockey Association the following fall.

Back at the Hippodrome on Friday, February 10th, Vaughan would earn his third shutout of the season, blanking the Chicago Yacht Club 4-0. The Yacht Club's claim to notoriety, even into the 21st century, is sponsorship of an annual race up Lake Michigan to Mackinac Island which was first held in 1898. Against Vaughan however, they were treading water, with all 26 of their shots turned away. Waterloo's offense was slowed somewhat by the absence of Keyes, who was suffering from flu. However, Richardson, Paul Berkey, and Charley Yount took advantage of extra ice time. Berkey scored twice on assists by Richardson, while Yount and Willey recorded the other markers.

Now with a 9-0 record, word was spreading about the success of hockey in Waterloo. The next week, Ed Brucher received a letter from the Legion's Department Commander, G. Decker French in Davenport:

> I wish someday I would get a letter containing a note that that bloomin' hockey team of yours has got licked. It seems almost lacking in sportsmanship to win every contest. Don't your players have any consideration for the other fellow? It is certainly a wonderful record you are hanging up, and this is just a way of saying "Hooray and keep it going."

Had someone actually wished ill toward the Waterloo team, they might have anticipated the looming matchups which would complete the February schedule. Similarly, if there was ever an occasion for a newspaper headline to tout the importance of an upcoming game or the quality of an incoming opponent, that time had arrived near the end of the 1927/28 season. The Legion expected sports fans from all over Iowa to make their way to Waterloo for the first international hockey game in state history.

OLYMPIANS AND PROFESSIONALS

The Becker-Chapman Legion hockey club was not a member of any league. As an entirely independent organization, the squad never had a formal schedule of games, regular matchups versus a circuit of regional rivals, nor the chance to represent Waterloo for a true championship of any kind. Those drawbacks could not outbalance the virtues of the team's situation in 1928.

Among the blessings which came with independence was the opportunity to meet opponents at varying levels of skill. When organizers began to promote the sport, they pitted the local team against foes who seemed likely to provide healthy opposition, without being unbeatable. Roy Malcolm's skaters proved repeatedly that they could match up well against squads assembled – as the Legion team was itself – from men who worked during the day, then took the ice nights and weekends. By mid-February, 1928, the Becker-Chapman Post had a nearly perfect record versus industrial or club teams, dating back to the first game at the Hippodrome almost exactly a year before.

The Legion Team

There was optimism beginning early in the 1927/28 season that Waterloo might find its most intriguing challenge yet by hosting a high quality opponent from college hockey. It was hoped that either the University of Wisconsin or Minnesota might be coaxed to send its squad to visit the Cedar Valley. In an era where a small percentage of Midwestern colleges sponsored varsity hockey and few had the financial capacity to send their teams to New England for games versus schools from the northeast, schedules were filled out with the competition which was available. The Badgers and Gophers each faced club and semiprofessional teams in the 1920's. In 1929, both crossed sticks with the same Chicago Athletic Association team which had become familiar to Waterloo fans. The Legion would eventually meet college teams, but sadly the dream of facing the undergraduates from Madison or St. Paul was never realized.

Another substantial benefit of not being confined within a league was the opportunity to play every game at the Cattle Congress grounds. The Becker-Chapman Post never had to pay for its own travel expenses, because there was no necessity to leave town. Every date which held the promise for a large crowd could be a home game, weather permitting, and as long as a visiting team was available from somewhere. Fans did not have to spend any time trying to follow their team's latest road results; they just needed to show up at the home rink.

In return for playing Waterloo with no chance for a reciprocal engagement, visiting organizations were compensated financially. The Legion set aside approximately $300 per game for opponents. After subtracting for railway tickets and other expenses, the balance was generally divided among the opposing players, who were likely to have been more cheerful about the prospect of traveling, meeting a strong Waterloo club, and occasionally being subjected to hometown officiating, thanks to the money they could bring back from the trip. Approximately one-third of the costs for staging a game at this time were related to the other team; Waterloo players split roughly $250 per matchup among themselves, with an additional $100 for Hippodrome rental, $100 for game promotion, and miscellaneous items accounting for another $150, making the total expense around $900.

From the beginning of the Legion's hockey project, teams from Minnesota and other colder areas had wanted to visit the Cedar Valley. During the same time that the details were being arranged for the very first game versus the Des Moines Old Pals, there was speculation about future games against aggregations from places like Winona, Rochester, and the Twin Cities. The Becker-Chapman hockey committee believed that better opponents were good for business, so long as the games remained competitive. Announcing the January, 1928 ticket price increase, the *Courier* explained this opinion, saying that promoters felt it was, "…better to raise the price of admission and continue the present schedule of high class hockey matches than to continue at the present admission prices and revert to the low-cost 'Iowa League' games for which they were established."

The perception that a strong opponent yielded a large crowd seems to have been borne out by Waterloo's first meetings with teams from St. Paul and Chicago, each of which drew 3,000 fans or more. The civic pride of facing and beating visiting clubs from such large cities where the sport enjoyed a more deeply-rooted following may have been a factor which helped attendance. So too was the promotion of each game as the biggest yet. There was talk in January 1928 of bringing a Canadian senior team to the Hippodrome from Ontario, or perhaps from Clarence Keyes' former hometown in Saskatchewan. When all the arrangements were concluded and a club from north of the border was eventually secured in February, they came from Winnipeg, and their arrival did help to draw some of the largest crowds in Becker-Chapman hockey history.

* * *

The Winnipeg Buffaloes boarded a train for Waterloo around midday on Tuesday, February 14th. Like the Hawks in Waterloo, the Buffaloes were a team without a league. When the Tammany Athletic Club did not sponsor hockey in the Manitoba Senior League, the Club's former "Tigers" came together in late November, 1927 to reconstitute themselves as the Buffaloes. However, uncertain membership caused the entire Manitoba loop to shut down for the winter, scattering many of the Buffaloes into Winnipeg's Big Four League, a circuit whose teams were sponsored by Canada's two major railroads – Canadian Pacific and Canadian National – and the city's largest department stores – Eaton's and the Hudson Bay Company. Big Four games at Winnipeg's Amphitheatre Rink were attended by crowds of 5,000 or more during the league's short schedule. Other members of the barnstorming Buffaloes squad who headed to Iowa were skaters from the Winnipeg Junior Hockey League. Traces of the team can still be found in the Canadian hockey record books.

The initial Winnipeg roster forwarded to the Legion included forwards Alston "Stoney" Wise and Romeo Rivers, both with the Eaton's that winter. Wise was 23, only five years removed from winning the Memorial Cup – Canada's highest junior hockey honor – while skating for the University of Manitoba. He had been playing at the senior level since 1923/24. Rivers was just shy of his 20th birthday and coming off a strong final season in juniors for the Elmwood Millionaires.

Wise and Rivers would be teammates again beginning in the 1929/30 season, with another local club known as the Winnipegs. In February 1931, the "Pegs" defeated the Hamilton Tigers for the Allan Cup, making them the top team in Canadian senior hockey. In that era, the Allan Cup champion was also awarded the right to represent Canada during the following year's World Championships or, every four years, at the Olympics. As a result, the Winnipegs spent the 1931/32 season preparing for the Winter Games – which would be held in Lake Placid, New York during February, 1932 – and hoping to maintain their nation's dominance for a fourth consecutive Olympic hockey tournament.

The Winnipegs were nicknamed the "Scoreless Wonders," and their style was summed up in a contemporary edition of the *Regina Leader-Post*, which noted that they "…are a lightning fast team, a great team defensively, but they lack scoring punch." Canada's previous Olympic entries had blasted European opponents by double-digit margins, but the results from Lake Placid were relatively closer. The Winnipegs even needed overtime to edge the United States, 2-1, during their first meeting in the double round-robin-formatted Olympic tournament.

The gold medal was up for grabs when the sides met again nine days later. The Americans had to win the game to tie the standings, which would force a one-game playoff.

During the second period, the U.S. took a 2-1 lead and held that score into the final minute of the third. With 43 seconds remaining, Rivers was inside the American blue line along the boards and sent a desperate shot toward the net. It knuckled through and around traffic, past goalie Frank Farrell, and across the goal line into the cage. Canada held out through the last seconds of regulation and overtime for a 2-2 final, maintaining their two-point advantage in the tournament standings and winning gold.

Almost exactly four years after having skated in Waterloo, Wise appeared in five of the six contests during the Lake Placid Olympics. He recorded two goals. However, Rivers seems to have missed the trip to the Cedar Valley. If he was actually aboard the train which carried the Buffaloes to Waterloo in 1928, he was not credited for stepping onto the Hippodrome ice in any box score.

A veteran of an earlier Olympic tournament appears to have been a late addition to the Buffaloes' Waterloo expedition, perhaps replacing Rivers. Harold McMunn had been included on Canada's 1924 national team when the Allan Cup champion Toronto Granites needed to bulk up their shorthanded lineup before traveling to Chamonix, France to claim the gold medal. Prior to that experience, in 1921 McMunn had won the Memorial Cup as a winger with the Winnipeg Falcons. His teammate during that championship effort was defenseman Sammy McCallum, who was with the Eaton's in 1928 and also aboard the train to Iowa.

Two other Buffaloes defensemen – members of the Hudson Bays during the Big Four League season – would later be affiliates of NHL teams. Norm Pridham signed with the Pittsburgh (hockey) Pirates in 1929, but spent most of his long professional career during the 1930's skating for teams west of the Rocky Mountains. Jim Arnott won three Pacific Coast Hockey League championships with the Vancouver Lions and later had connections to the New York Rangers. Neither player ultimately reached the National Hockey League.

Goaltender Bert White was another Big Four Leaguer. With Pridham and Arnott, White had moved to the Hudson Bay's in 1927/28 after previously appearing for the Tammany Tigers senior club in 1926/27. All three played at Tammany AC with center Art Shaw, who was also traveling with the Buffaloes. Shaw had been a two-sport athlete for the Tigers and taken the field with them as they made an unsuccessful bid for the 1925 Grey Cup, which at the time was awarded to the top Canadian rugby club before any version of American-style football had taken hold north of the border. Additional members of the Winnipeg delegation to Waterloo included tough guy Tono McDonald, and juniors Fred Jennings and Stew Musgrove.

Winnipeg's trip to Waterloo began only after some tense moments for the Legion hockey committee. Warm weather had brought on a thaw, and there was concern that the sloppy travel conditions might make it difficult to draw the number of spectators post officials were hoping to attract. There was discussion at a Monday night committee meeting about whether to proceed with the Waterloo-Winnipeg games as scheduled for Wednesday, the 15th, and Friday, the 17th, or to postpone the Buffaloes and find another opponent for a Friday night tilt. A forecast for cooler weather helped convince the committee to go ahead with their original plan, and on this occasion, the weather would cooperate. The Legion also made arrangements to have two dozen men manage the Dairy Cattle Congress parking areas to make sure the scores of expected vehicles would be arranged properly. In the Hippodrome, extra water was pushed off the ice surface Tuesday, and anticipation built for the games.

The Buffaloes rolled into Waterloo, pulled by a Chicago Great Western Railway locomotive, after spending a full day and night in transit. Much of their luggage did not arrive with them, so with just a few hours remaining before game time, they headed from the train station to the Hippodrome without any jerseys. Fortunately, the old uniforms which the Legion had recently replaced were still available. There must have been at least a few confused spectators murmuring and staring when two teams in Becker-Chapman colors took the ice for the playing of "The Star Spangled Banner" and Canada's "God Save the King" beneath Old Glory and the Union Jack.

After the national anthems, referee Roy Westphalinger was ready to drop the puck for the 8:15 contest. Westphalinger was a St. Paul native, brought to Waterloo to oversee the series after playing against the Hawks with the Hook 'em Cows and Cowboys earlier in the winter. Nearly 19 minutes of scoreless hockey followed the opening faceoff as the crowd of 3,000 looked on. Then with just under 90 seconds remaining in the first period, Earle Willey sent a shot toward the net. White stopped it but left a rebound, and Clarence Keyes – back from his bout with the flu – knocked it in for the opening goal of the game.

The lead lasted only a minute-and-a-half into the second period before Wise tied the score. However, from then onward Waterloo goalie Bill Vaughan was unbeatable. He made 25 saves during the contest "…at least half of which were so sensational that the crowd roared its approval," according to the *Courier*'s postgame account. At the other end of the ice, White proved to be just as difficult to contend with, until Willey finally solved him for the decisive score, set up by Paul Berkey with just over seven minutes remaining in regulation. The Legion held on to edge the travel-weary Buffaloes, 2-1.

Winnipeg moved into the Russell-Lamson Hotel at the corner of Fifth and Commercial Streets, hoping to recover from their long train ride and the physical first game in Waterloo. Thursday, they were lunch guests of the Lions Club, where Mayor Glenn Tibbitts gave them a more friendly welcome to the community than they had received on the ice the previous evening. Speculation abounded that rest for the Buffaloes, combined with even faster ice Friday, would make it unlikely for the Hawks to duplicate their performance.

Nonetheless, a great deal of excitement about the Friday rematch brought 4,500 people to the Hippodrome. They waited just over two minutes before the Legion jumped ahead. Keyes sent a shot toward White, who fought it off. The resulting rebound gave Louis Webber the opportunity he needed to knock in the first score, the only goal during the first period.

Webber was in his mid-20's during the winter of 1928. He had been born in Springfield, Illinois, but his family moved to White Bear Lake, Minnesota, during his youth. He began playing hockey there, learning the game by watching the village's hockey hero Frank "Moose" Goheen, at the time an amateur player in St. Paul, later a member of the 1920 U.S. Olympic team, and eventually an honoree of the Hockey Hall of Fame in 1952. In the early 1920's, Webber had the opportunity to play against Goheen in an exhibition pitting young players against old timers from the community, presented by White Bear Lake's American Legion Post. Webber and his young White Bear teammates also faced club teams from St. Paul, the College of St. Thomas, and anyone else interested in taking the ice on chilly January and February days.

The talkative Webber enjoyed recounting his war adventures in France to new friends in Waterloo. After enlisting in the year after the United States joined the conflict, the teenager was assigned to serve with an engineering company supporting the American Expeditionary Force. Posted first in Massachusetts, then Virginia, Webber made the crossing to Europe in the late spring of 1918, and spent the closing months of the war behind the Allied lines. According to Webber's story, with his exact whereabouts unknown to his family, they contacted the Army to find him and send him home, which was accomplished only after some difficulty in late 1919 or early 1920.

Webber's companion during his time in France was apparently none other than Paul Castner, a St. Paul native who became an All-American football player at Notre Dame in the early 1920's, served as player/coach for the Fighting Irish hockey team, and then appeared in a half dozen major league baseball games for the Chicago White Sox in 1923. Webber – who also was a boxer during at least one White Bear Lake Legion event – shared Castner's enthusiasm for baseball as well. Just a few weeks before Waterloo's series with the Buffaloes, the forward had been offered a tryout to play infield for the Waterloo Hawks when the local baseball team took the field in the spring. Webber, a shortstop on the diamond, didn't make that roster, going instead to Rochester,

Minnesota, to play for and coach a semiprofessional club there over the summer, until returning to Waterloo for the 1928/29 hockey season.

The goal which Webber scored in the second game against the Buffaloes stood up as Winnipeg fired 24 shots at Vaughan "...who covered himself in glory and bruises" during the first two periods. Then with under a minute remaining before the second intermission, Keyes stepped away from the boards with the puck, navigated through three defenders, and knocked a shot past White. The Buffaloes sliced the lead back to a single goal at 1:48 of the third as Shaw capitalized on a chance created by McMunn. However, Roy Malcolm delivered the next goal with five-and-a-half minutes remaining, firing a long shot off White's stick and into the net. Keyes then sprinted into the Buffaloes' defensive zone to score at 17:34, sealing the 4-1 victory with his third point of the night.

Rather than boarding their train for home, the Buffaloes were still in Waterloo Saturday morning.

"We're not convinced yet that we can't beat this Waterloo team," announced Winnipeg coach Dave Johnston colorfully. "We've beat a lot of good ones in our time and we think we've been under a hoodoo down here. The next game will be a grudge game."

That morning, a third matchup was arranged for Monday, the 20th. The Winnipeg players stayed two more nights, practicing Sunday afternoon. Both teams were guests at another civic luncheon on Monday, this time sponsored by the local Rotary Club. Despite his defiant tone, Johnston admitted that the Canadians were impressed with their visit, telling the *Courier*, "Our stay in Waterloo has been a most pleasant experience…We are leaving tonight…with a feeling that we could not be been treated better anywhere in the world. And that goes regardless, whether we win or lose the third game with your splendid hockey team..."

Waterloo and Winnipeg found their way back to Cattle Congress and were joined by an audience of 2,500 for the almost-impromptu meeting that night. The "grudge game" began as the first matchup had the previous Wednesday, with no score for most of the first period. Just before intermission, Shaw snapped a shot toward the net, forcing a Vaughan save. However, the former rugby player found his own rebound and scored on the second chance. For the first time during the entire 1927/28 season, the Legion skaters found themselves playing from behind.

In the second, Waterloo's determined effort to even the game was thwarted as White turned away 14 shots. Instead of the Hawks making the tally 1-1, Winnipeg added to their margin when Jennings scored at 6:24. The Legion continued to press in the third, leading to a defensive breakdown at 13:48. Jennings carried the puck into the Waterloo zone for a two-on-none breakaway, and Vaughan was unable to deny Shaw his second goal of the contest as Jennings delivered the puck to his linemate for the easy marker. Celebrating their 3-0 victory, the Buffaloes departed for home at 2 a.m. Waterloo's season-long eleven-game winning streak had ended. On top of that, the Legion players knew that an even tougher opponent would be chugging up the Great Western tracks from the opposite direction the following week.

* * *

The Twin Cities were the hub of the American Hockey Association during the late 1920's. Minneapolis and St. Paul each had a club in the professional league, and from there players could catch a train to northern outposts in Winnipeg and Duluth. During 1926/27, the circuit had included a Chicago entry, the Cardinals, whose lone season coincided with the Chicago Black Hawks' debut in the NHL. The Cardinals limped to the end of the AHA schedule in last place, and owner Edward Livingstone alleged that Black Hawks founder Frederic McLaughlin had ruined his business and swiped several of his players. Lawyers sorted out the dispute in court during the winter of 1927/28, while the remnant of the Cardinals team moved to Kansas City and became the Pla-Mors. It's likely that the Pla-Mors rode the rails north through Waterloo aboard *The Tri-State* or *Mills Cities Limited* trains to Minnesota and Manitoba on their way to nearly every road game against league opponents during their first season.

Defenseman Jim Seaborn and winger Roy "Gloomy" Lessard were among the former Cardinals on Kansas City's 1927/28 team. Lessard had also been a star with the Sault Ste. Marie Greyhounds and won an Allan Cup with the club in 1924. Seaborn's exploits were even more notable. As early as 1914/15, he had appeared with the Vancouver Millionaires in the Pacific Coast Hockey Association at a time when the PCHA's best team had the opportunity to play for the Stanley Cup each year. In fact, the Millionaires claimed the Cup in 1915, winning a series against the Ottawa Senators of the NHA (predecessor to the NHL). Seaborn's name is engraved with those of his teammates inside the bowl atop the trophy. Born in 1890, he played in Minnesota after The World War and continued his professional career in the United States into the 1930's.

Joe McCormick was another Pla-Mor with big league credentials. In the first half of the 1920's, he had appeared with the Edmonton Eskimos and Portland Rosebuds in the Western Canada and Western Hockey Leagues respectively. Like the PCHA, the WCHL and WHL had the right to play the NHL champ for the Stanley Cup before the circuits went out of business. Born in Buckingham, Quebec, McCormick had also been on the ice during the first Olympic Games in which hockey was played, as captain of the *United States* team. The 1920 Antwerp Olympics offered a return visit to Europe for McCormick, who had served with U.S. Armed Forces during the war. His enlistment helped provide him with the U.S. citizenship necessary to later be part of the 1920 National Team, after having arrived in Pittsburgh to play hockey there prior to the United States' entry into the conflict.

The Pla-Mors' Leo Lafrance had spent most of 1927/28 in the National Hockey League. After a brief stint with the Montreal Canadiens a year earlier, the forward split nearly 30 games between Montreal and the Chicago Black Hawks in '27/28 before being sent to Kansas City to finish the winter. Lafrance had run into trouble in Montreal after going AWOL from the club at one point. Following his transfer to the Play-Mors, he would never return to the NHL, although he enjoyed considerable success in the AHA and other minor leagues.

Conversely, defenseman Duke Dukowski was on his way up. Like McCormick, Dukowski had several seasons of experience in the west, and like Lafrance, he had made his NHL debut in 1926/27. The first-generation Polish immigrant had played in 28 of the Chicago Black Hawks' 44 games during their first season. Following two years in Kansas City, Dukowski would return to the Black Hawks in 1929/30, serving as team captain, appearing in every game, and scoring a career-best seven goals and 17 points. All totaled, he dressed for 200 NHL games with the Hawks, New York Americans, and New York Rangers before retiring in 1934. Dukowski's nephew, Brian – also nicknamed "Duke," but who spelled his last name "Dutkowski" – would come to Waterloo a generation later. The younger "Duke" was a member of the United States Hockey League's Waterloo Black Hawks of the 1960's, also working as a teacher and coach at Columbus High School.

Approaching the final weeks of the 1927/28 season, the Pla-Mors were tangled in a tight AHA race. Dukowski, Lessard, and forward Pete Mitchell had all been battling injuries but were coming back to full health. The Pla-Mors held fourth place in the five-team league during late February, trailing the Duluth Hornets, St. Paul Saints, and Minneapolis Millers. Kansas City edged the Saints 3-2 in a rough game at home on Sunday, February 26th and climbed into a third place tie. Five AHA games remained on the Pla-Mors schedule, beginning with a contest on the 29th in Minneapolis. Kansas City players boarded a train late Monday night and arrived in Waterloo the next morning to prepare for an exhibition against the Becker-Chapman club before their next important league game.

There were practical reasons for the Pla-Mors to visit Waterloo for a matchup at such a crucial time in their season. Playing the Waterloo club was a matter of convenience at a natural stopping point. The game represented an opportunity to raise a few extra dollars as the schedule wound to a close. Plus, Kansas City officials were hoping to see goaltender Bill Vaughan and defenseman Bob Collette in action.

Vaughan and Collette were good friends who had played

together in Minnesota. The goalie had helped convince the defenseman to join the Waterloo team instead of playing in Michigan's Upper Peninsula during the fall of 1927. At 23 and in his first season on the squad, Collette was named Waterloo's captain. A White Bear Lake, Minnesota, native like Louis Webber, he had also been awed in his youth by local star Moose Goheen. Collette had built a reputation as a defenseman with scoring touch while playing with his classmates from the St. Mary's Parish school and for the White Bear Junior Athletic Club. Quick, but not big, he looked the part of a hockey player by the time he arrived in the Cedar Valley, with several prominent gold teeth replacing the originals which had been lost at the rink. Not all of his teeth had been knocked out by sticks or pucks either; Collette was one of the toughest players the Legion ever signed and squared off with opponents in several notable scraps.

Bob even fought his younger brother, Gene, on at least one memorable occasion, as the *Waterloo Courier* related in January, 1929:

> Bob had been playing on a team north of Minneapolis which had made a splendid record – so good that all of Minnesota's semipro teams would not schedule a game. Bob attempted to schedule a game with Gene and the White Bear Lake team, which had likewise enjoyed a successful year, but Gene was leery, and refused to sign for the contest. But where there's a will there's a way, and Bob opened negotiations with Gene under a nom de plume [assumed name] and under the pretense that he was a negro gentleman, representing the only negro hockey team in captivity. Gene fell for the idea and signed. The ballyhoo was started and all White Bear Lake was present when the enemy arrived for the contest.

Jet black after hours of work with paint, Bob's team skated out on the rink to play the white gentlemen from White Bear Lake.

But Gene thought something was wrong – these negro boys played too much like boys he knew and had played with and against. He investigated; became sure of himself: called a conference of the home boys and the war was on. Then the police arrived.

Up at White Bear Lake the natives still talk about the hockey game and free-for-all fight staged by the home team and the negro squad.

Their differences settled by early 1928, Gene joined Bob in Waterloo briefly at the end of the season. He appeared during the final game versus the Winnipeg Buffaloes while the Hawks were shorthanded, but became sick and returned home in the week before the Pla-Mors came to town.

The 2,000 locals who turned out for the Tuesday night game against Kansas City saw the Legion take the ice without center Clarence Keyes, who was ill once again and removed from the lineup shortly before the opening faceoff. They also saw a visiting team which looked far different from any of the post's previous opponents. As the newspaper recounted the following day, "Beside the massive visitors, the Waterloo players looked like midgets." Still, Waterloo struck first, just over four minutes into the action. Starting forwards Webber and Brock Richardson moved the puck into the offensive zone, setting up Earle Willey for the score.

Waterloo's lead lasted less than four minutes. Dutkowski assisted on a goal by Pla-Mors' top scorer, Ken Dunfield. Thirty seconds later, Kansas City took the lead for good. Attempting to kick the puck away from his net, Collette redirected it into his own goal. Early in the second, the visitors added to their lead with a marker by Garnet Campbell. Dutkowski scored for the Pla-Mors at 12:31. By the end of regulation, the tally stood at 6-1. Vaughan likely did not leave the impression he might have hoped to make, stopping 22 of the 28 chances directed his way. Legion players managed only 18 shots against Pat Byrne.

Kansas City lost a 1-0 game to Minneapolis the next night. However, the Pla-Mors would still finish strongly, rallying to second place in the AHA during the final weeks of the season. Meanwhile, the Becker-Chapman hockey committee made plans for the last game of the campaign to be played the weekend following the Kansas City matchup. What they didn't know as they left the Hippodrome Tuesday night was that they would meet a different opponent than they were anticipating.

* * *

Two months earlier, members of the Augsburg College hockey team might have expected that early March would find them closer to the Waterloo in Belgium – site of decisive 1815 battle between Napoleon and the British – than its namesake community in northeast Iowa. When their plans for the winter changed, the squad was briefly slated to visit the Cedar Valley for the final Legion game of the season. Augsburg is a small Lutheran school in Minneapolis, and in early 1928, just a few hundred students were enrolled there. Five of them were brothers named Hanson. "The Hansons of Augsburg" played five of the six starting positions for the school's hockey team and had been chosen by the United States Amateur Hockey Association to represent the nation at the 1928 Olympics in St. Moritz,

Switzerland.

At 28 years old, Julius was the eldest of the Hanson's and leader of the group. Oscar was the youngest at 19, with Joe, Emil, and Louis in between. Goaltender Moose Swanson was the only player in the lineup who was not related. Together, they helped make Augsburg one of the best college hockey teams in the western United States at that time.

The Pittsburgh-based USAHA sought to send a full team as its Olympic representative – much like the Canadians, who automatically nominated their Allan Cup champion – rather than a collection of top players from several different teams. However, it was difficult to find volunteers for the honor, due to the cost of traveling to Europe. According to the *Pittsburgh Post-Gazette*, "...the Augsburg team in Minneapolis had worked hard to comply with the stipulations of the hockey committee, including the provision that half of the expenses of the trip abroad must be defrayed by the team or its sponsors..." Several thousand dollars were raised for the project, and the team prepared to travel to New York, sail on January 25th, and arrive in time for the games in early February.

A week before their departure, bad news arrived. General Douglas MacArthur, head of the AAU's Olympic Committee in New York, vetoed Augsburg's selection. Politics between the USAHA and AAU were part of the problem. In a telegram to Hockey Association leader William Haddock, reprinted by the Associated Press, MacArthur explained that the Olympic Committee's decision to send no U.S. team at all had been made on January 10th, and the USAHA's formal nomination of Augsburg hadn't arrived until January 17th. He also cited the fact no games had been played to determine who would represent the United States, saying "...open competition is the standard by which the Olympic committee determines its teams and without such basis it does not feel it can approve your recommendation." An offer by the University Club of Boston to play an exhibition game against Augsburg to clear up this point was rejected, due to a lack of time to make arrangements. Finally, MacArthur was widely quoted as saying that Augsburg was "not a representative team." Whether that was because a tryout or tournament had not been held, because the Hanson's were brothers and all shared the same Scandinavian ancestry, or because they had been raised for at least part of their youth in Camrose, Alberta – as was revealed after the furor started – is unclear. Ultimately, the United States did not field a hockey team in the 1928 Winter Olympics, from Augsburg or anywhere else.

With the "Auggies" thus available, the Becker-Chapman hockey committee went to work in an effort to bring them to Waterloo. The game was scheduled for Friday, March 2nd, the same week as the matchup versus the Pla-Mors. The *Courier* announced the opponent, remarking, "All are burly fellows, well versed in the ice sport and undefeated in three seasons. They have been mopping up on the best the northwest has to offer, and if the Hawks are still crippled it may mean another setback." Despite a tendency toward exaggeration, the paper may have actually been giving the Hanson's their due credit. Emil and Oscar would both reach the NHL during the 1930's, with the Detroit Red Wings and Chicago Black Hawks respectively.

Just as Augsburg supporters had been disappointed by the Olympic Committee's decision, so now it was Waterloo's turn to miss out. The day before the game was to be played, it was announced that Augsburg athletic director Si Melby had canceled the matchup. No explanation for the change was ever reported. In lieu of the near-national team, the Legion scrambled to recall the soldiers of Fort Snelling. With Clarence Keyes still out sick, it was expected that the Fort Snelling squad, which had stayed within two goals of Waterloo in the earlier meeting, might have the chance to even the series.

More than 25 minutes went by in the Friday night season finale before Earle Willey broke the scoreless tie. Louis Webber made it 2-0 a minute later. The soldiers scored midway through the period, but Waterloo took a commanding 5-1 lead to the second intermission, thanks to a natural hat trick by Paul Berkey, completed in a four-minute span. The Legion ended up winning by a final score of 8-1, allowing Fort Snelling just a dozen shots on goal.

Early the following week, the Becker-Chapman Post held a banquet for the team at Black's Tea Room. It was a season worth celebrating. Waterloo's hockey club had claimed twelve of 14 games, never trailing in the dozen contests they won. Early in the schedule, they had dominated the three teams they had met in close contests a season before. The Legion players had defeated opponents from the big cities of Chicago and Minneapolis. They won two of three games against a Winnipeg team full of notable players, and hosted the professional Pla-Mors in a game which might have been closer had Waterloo been able to dress a fully healthy lineup.

It was announced that hockey would return to Waterloo the following winter. Many of the Legion players were impressed enough by the 1927/28 results to come back. Over 30,000 fans had made their way to Cattle Congress to see the Hawks. The local support had helped the Becker-Chapman Post return a profit of $2,800 on their ice investment. By all indications, it appeared that hockey in the Hippodrome would become a permanent feature of the winter landscape in the Cedar Valley.

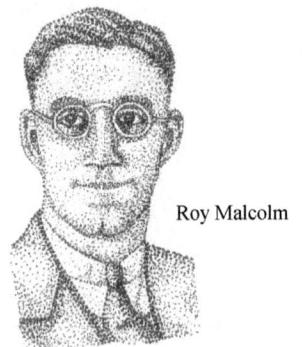 Roy Malcolm

 Fred Wagner

Postcard featuring the National Cattle Congress Hippodrome, from the collection of Brandon J. Brockway.

 Earle Willey

 Bill Vaughan

The Legion Team

West 4th Street looking toward the YMCA and the Cedar River, circa 1928, from the archives of The Grout Museum of History and Science, Waterloo, IA.

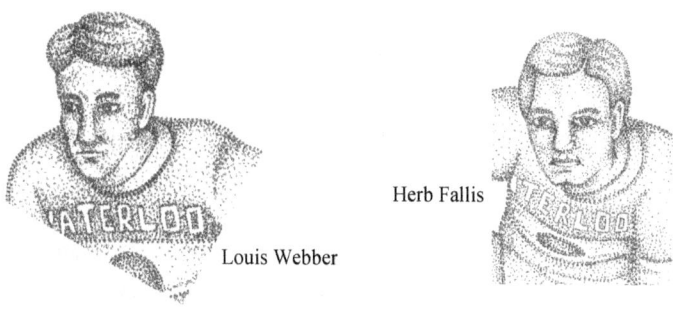

Louis Webber

Herb Fallis

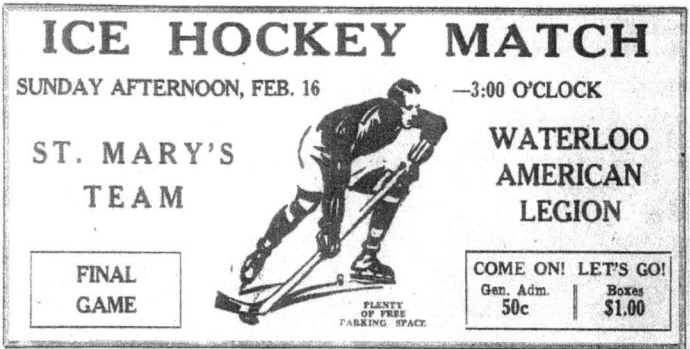

Advertisement for the last game of the 1929/30 hockey season.

A SERVICE TO THE COMMUNITY

John Deere doubled the size of its Waterloo production facilities in 1928. The company spent over a million dollars and hired more than 600 construction workers to complete the project, without slowing the assembly lines at its factory campus located between the Dairy Cattle Congress grounds and downtown. Cedar Valley natives had been building mechanized agricultural equipment since the Waterloo Gasoline Traction Engine Company was founded in 1892. By the end of 1928, 3,000 locals – a workforce which had more than doubled since 1925 – took a daily shift in one of the huge buildings on the 75 acres once known as Mullan's Pasture.

In the late 1920's, Deere was unveiling its General Purpose, or "GP," model tractor. In advertisements, the company bragged that the machine could handle a variety of chores around the farm. With it, a farmer could plant or cultivate three rows of corn at a time, working 30 to 40 acres of land in a single day. Waterloo-produced tractors generated $25 million for the company in 1928.

"The past year has been very good for the sale of power farm equipment," Allen Head, General Manager of John Deere's Waterloo operations, announced in December. "The general crop situation this year has been encouraging, with the money returns to the farmer better than in 1927. Prospects for 1929 are better than for many years."

As productive as the tractor works was, by revenue it was not the biggest business in the community. Across the Cedar River and on the other side of town, Rath Packing processed over $30 million dollars of meat. In the closing days of 1928, they slaughtered their one millionth hog, up from 842,000 a year earlier. Rath's 2,000 employees prepared pork and beef for people throughout the United States and exported it to 57 other countries.

Many other businesses on both sides of the Cedar River were busy in the postwar years. Waterloo workers built refrigerators, fashioned caskets, and manufactured cosmetics. Altstadt & Langlas baked Kleen-Made brand bread, and the Waterloo Canning Company shipped six million cans of sweet corn each year. Armstrong Manufacturing assembled rigs for drilling oil and water wells, while Monarch Film Company produced educational movies and advertising pieces. Beginning in 1908, Gem Doughnut Manufacturing Company had made the equipment for bakeries and diners to fry millions of doughnuts.

With such an industrious business atmosphere, Waterloo was growing. Three hundred, twenty-seven new houses were built in 1928. Nearly 1,000 new vehicles were registered in the city, with Black Hawk County residents in possession of 17,000 cars and trucks by the end of the year. Travelers could come to and from Waterloo even faster in the fall after Chapman Field was opened; fighter pilot Eddie

Rickenbacker, the nation's most famous aerial hero of the war, was on hand when the airfield east of Waterloo on Grant Highway was christened in honor of Waterloo's own air corps hero, Carl Chapman. Six days each week, flights buzzed back and forth from Des Moines on a regular schedule.

Residents in the prosperous community were looking forward to another promising hockey season as 1928 waned and players began returning to the Cedar Valley in late November. Team manager Roy Malcolm organized the squad for its third season, planning to play again on a limited basis as a reserve defenseman. Center Clarence Keyes was named captain. The White Bear Lake contingent of Louis Webber, Bob Collette, and younger brother Gene Collette all made their way back to town, as did forward Brock Richardson. Winger Earle Willey had nearly earned a place on the Kansas City Pla-Mors' roster, but by the first week of December, he was living in Cedar Falls and looking for a day job along with many of his teammates.

Additions to the team included Cameron MacKinnon, a husky defenseman from Edmonton who had served with Canadian forces during the war. Besides minding the area around the Waterloo net, MacKinnon also assisted in maintaining the Hippodrome ice rink and sold sporting goods at Black Hawk Sports Shop. Bill Hunter returned to Waterloo after playing for the Legion briefly in 1927, a stint which included scoring the first goal team history. In the interim, he had been skating for the Old Pals Athletic Club in Des Moines, working at a bank there, and attending Capital City Commercial College. Becker-Chapman officials also snagged Sgt. Steve Mickey, who had played against Waterloo for Fort Snelling and forward Ralph Gorr, who came from Drinkwater, Saskatchewan, the same town where Keyes had formerly skated.

Goaltending was an area of some uncertainty as the players congregated. Bill Vaughan had joined the American Hockey Association's new St. Louis Flyers. However, with little prospect of becoming the Flyers' starting goalie, he decided his chances might be better returning to Waterloo. Vaughan wrote Malcolm about the decision in the closing days of November and arrived in time for the first on-ice practice. Not fully healthy, Vaughan was unable to even reclaim his job in the Waterloo net.

Anticipating that his 1927/28 star netminder would be playing professional hockey, Malcolm had made arrangements months earlier to import 27-year-old Jack Hand. Like Malcolm, Hand was from Red Deer, Alberta, and Malcolm's brother had recommended him for the apparently open Waterloo roster slot. The dark-haired, blue-eyed Hand said he had become a goaltender, because he wasn't fast enough for any other position. On the ice, he found his calling between the pipes and was dependable. Away from the rink, the graduate of St. John's Technical High School in Winnipeg went to work in the repair department at John Deere.

During the first days of December, ice at the Hippodrome was not yet ready, although work was underway to freeze and build up the playing surface. For conditioning purposes, players went to the YMCA. Over two hours each evening, they played volleyball, basketball, and tossed around a medicine ball. Cold weather at the time had some even trudging out to test the strength of the outdoor ice at Cedar River Park lagoon.

The first game of the season was scheduled for Friday,

December 14th against the Minnesota Mining and Manufacturing Company team from Minneapolis, and the Cattle Congress rink was declared ready for practice the Sunday before. Local fans were so enthusiastic for the start of the season, some turned out for the morning scrimmage. It was during that initial practice that the club suffered its first setback of the early season. Skating through some sawdust which was on the ice, Webber lost his balance, fell, and cut his leg severely enough to be taken to Allen Hospital for stitches. He was still there nearly a week later after developing a fever.

Like their injured winger, Webber's teammates didn't spend much additional time on the ice either. The squad practiced on Monday, but warm weather, described as "April-like," meant the rink began to thaw. At 9:30 Thursday morning, the Legion canceled the season opener versus 3M, setting sights instead on a matchup against St. Mary's College of Winona, Minnesota, on December 20th. Although more seasonal weather returned at the beginning of the new week, Malcolm bemoaned the state of the Hippodrome on the 19th, remarking, "An inspection of the ice this morning showed it to be bumpy and melted to the ground in places." The St. Mary's affair was called off too, and 3M was back at the top of the schedule for a Christmas Day contest.

In lieu of meeting St. Mary's, the team held a long workout after repairs to the playing surface. Practice continued throughout the weekend, including a double-session at 10 a.m. and 8:30 p.m. on Sunday the 23rd. In between, the Legion had one of its first opportunities of the season to open the rink up to local skaters for general use. Malcolm named his starting lineup on Christmas Eve, including Willey among the forwards. However, the arrival of the holiday saw the departure of the high-scoring forward. Following two cancelations and difficulty even finding ice to practice on, Willey left Waterloo for steadier opportunities back in Michigan's Upper Peninsula. The initial lineup needed even further revision before the game, with Webber placed in reserve after not fully recovering from his hospital stay.

The adversity appeared to be over 12:45 into the game when Bob Collette set up his brother, Gene, for the first goal into the new twine netting, which had been installed to replace the old wire mesh. Unfortunately, 3M goals by Elmer Nelson and Bill Halder before intermission swung the matchup the other way. Gorr tied the game early in the second period, but it only remained 2-2 for a little more than three minutes. Visiting goaltender "Rosy" Picha turned away the rest of Waterloo's chances, and 3M skated to a three-goal victory, 5-2. Less than 1,500 were on hand for the contest.

The final days of 1928 were no kinder to the Legion. Another matchup, slated for Friday the 28th versus the St. Paul Armour Packers, had to be called off because of warm weather and poor ice. Public skating was put on hold. During the limited ice time which was available to prepare for a New Year's Day game against the Minneapolis electrical workers of the W.B. Forshay Company, Webber was cut again (this time over his right eye), Keyes suffered bruised ribs, and Richardson sprained an arm. The air of invincibility Waterloo hockey enjoyed during the previous spring had most certainly abated.

* * *

Hockey had been exciting and profitable for the Becker-Chapman Post, but in late 1928, Legion officials in many of Iowa largest communities, including Waterloo, were thinking about another sport. The first boxing matches sponsored by Cedar Valley Legionnaires had been held early in the decade. By 1926, a series of fights – highlighted by a tilt between nationally-known heavyweight William "Young" Stribling and local favorite Lou Rollinger – helped generate a $1,400 profit for the post. The bouts continued into 1927 with the assistance of promoter Maurice Cohn. Fights in Waterloo were often staged at the National Guard Armory, Electric Park Ballroom, or the Hippodrome when a larger venue was required.

Unfortunately, Iowa had no sanctioning body to regulate boxing, and the sport was technically illegal in the state at the professional level. This presented problems, illustrated by an Armory fight card – promoted by Cohn, but which the Legion was not involved with – during February, 1928. Boxers from St. Paul, Chicago, and Des Moines made their way to the ring at the National Guard facility. Waterloo native Al Knipp delighted the crowd, winning a ten-round decision against up-and-coming scrapper Ken Hunt. It was the best of five bouts during the evening.

None of the 2,000 who saw the show paid for a ticket. Cohn and the other organizers decided at the last minute not charge admission for fear of legal repercussions. The Public Morals Committee of the Waterloo Ministerial Association had complained to the sheriff that, by law, the event should be stopped before the opening bell. Explaining their decision to interject themselves into the issue, the ministers argued that fighting shouldn't be promoted to impressionable young people, that the sport was vicious and without redeeming value, and that since there was a state law against prize fights, it shouldn't simply be ignored.

Morals Committee Chairman the Rev. Dr. Warren Steeves of Walnut Street Baptist Church did not temper his low opinion of those who congregated around the ring, saying, "In general the persons identified with boxing are not the persons who are making a valuable contribution to society."

Steeves and the other ministers were not amused when Cohn formally invited them to attend the Armory fight after their stance on the issue created the controversy.

As a result of the religious row, the promoters believed that their only option was to collect a voluntary offering from those in attendance, thus keeping it a technically amateur event. Fighter Hymie Wiseman reportedly had to borrow money to get home to Des Moines, while referee Alex Fidler went unpaid and even without reimbursement for his expenses. Other fight cards planned for the Armory later in the year were canceled.

At the American Legion's state convention, held in Cedar Rapids during November 1928, the organization decided to lobby the Iowa General Assembly to legalize boxing in 1929. Political action was not out of the ordinary for the Legion. Regularly the champions of veteran's issues at the Capitol, the group had a state-level legislative committee which helped to model bills, later introduced by friendly politicians each spring when lawmakers convened. The committee included the original commander of the Becker-Chapman Post, Harry Reed, who would later be appointed the U.S. District Attorney for Iowa's Northern Judicial District during the Hoover Administration.

The *Iowa Legionnaire* newsletter summarized the

organization's stance on fights, claiming, "Boxing is not as brutal as football or basketball. Nearly every college and high school in the state has these two sports. The American Legion, believing that, if properly conducted, boxing is quite as attractive as football, basketball, or any other sport, wants it to be under the law."

While there may have been a legitimate interest in promoting a contemporarily popular form of athletics, there was certainly a more pragmatic motive for the Legion to raise the boxing issue. If successful, the effort could provide a valuable revenue stream for local posts across the state, especially in larger communities. Kansas Legionnaires had persuaded their state to implement a boxing law earlier in the decade. From that success, the Iowa contingent had a ready-made blueprint for constructing their own bill.

"Prior to its enactment [in Kansas] all bouts were illegal, and most of them had certain distasteful features and characters," explained State Legion Commander George Prichard. "The Legion felt that the bill it submitted would remedy the evils, and the Iowa Legion, knowing that the same conditions exist here as existed in Kansas, wants to emulate the Kansas example."

The act intended to charter an Iowa boxing commission, responsible for creating the specific guidelines for fights. Beyond simply laying out a code for what was to happen in the ring, this sanctioning body would also be charged with watching out for the health and safety of participants, certifying referees, and making sure bouts were *on the level*. As proposed, the bill would also have levied a 10% state tax on all boxing gate receipts, and given local city and county governments autonomy to decide for themselves whether fights would be allowed in their communities.

Just prior to the end of 1928, Becker-Chapman boxing supporters landed a healthy public relations blow. Northern Illinois native Sammy Mandell had come to Waterloo for a bout in 1923, knocking out opponent Jimmy Mahoney. For the fighter whom the Associated Press later remembered "...was noted for his great comeback ability and often rallied for victory after seemingly on the verge of being badly beaten," the Waterloo tilt had been a step on the way to winning the World Lightweight Title at Chicago's Comiskey Park in 1926. Now in an interview with the *Waterloo Courier* published on Christmas Day, Mandell (who would remain lightweight champion until 1930) pledged to box in the Cedar Valley again if the Legion's prizefighting bill passed.

The article did not remind readers that only 18 months earlier, although it was determined to be no fault of the champion, Mandell's opponent Steve Adams had died in the ring after a second round knockdown. An unresponsive Adams received last rights from a priest while still lying on the canvas in front of the stunned crowd, and Mandell was taken into custody before appearing at a coroner's inquiry. The fateful event had been staged in Kansas City, Kansas.

* * *

The arrival of 1929 brought better fortune for Waterloo's hockey club, at least early in the first period of their New Year's Day game against Forshay of Minneapolis. Just over five minutes into the matchup, one of the visiting forwards knocked the puck into his own net to give the Hawks an edge. After the score was tied at the beginning of the second frame, Roy Malcolm sent the disk to Gene Collette for a goal at 15:20. Malcolm capitalized on a chance himself midway through the final period, and the Legion players claimed a 3-2 victory.

While the January 1st decision moved the Becker-Chapman team to 1-1 for the winter, January 2nd was a big day for the rest of the local hockey community. The City of Waterloo installed temporary lights and 16-inch dasher boards for outdoor evening hockey at Cedar River Park. In mid-December, five rinks had been laid out there by the Parks Department. Everything was now prepared for youth and industrial league hockey to commence.

The previous winter, Playground Director and Legionnaire Victor Reed had helped organize on-ice activities in the community, but it had been the end of January before the outdoor project was set in motion. While a handful of junior and adult recreational games were played, the big event planned for Cedar River Park in the winter of 1927/28 had been an Ice Derby in February. Warm weather forced postponement and relocation to the Hippodrome at the end of that month. Among the 200 skaters who participated, Russell Hackett was the big winner of the event, claiming a pair of silver skates. Reed was determined to get an earlier start in '28/29 and make the most what was available during the always unpredictable cycle of freeze and thaw.

Four teams were quick to sign up for the local industrial league's new season. They represented Rath Packing, Armstrong Manufacturing, Altstadt & Langlas Bakery, and Bain Dental Laboratories. By mid-January, the roster had swelled to include six more clubs from Mac's Pharmacy, Repass Automobile Company, Clute's Grocery, Black's department store, Illinois Central railroad, and John Deere.

In regards to youth hockey, the game was popular enough

to be found in the city beyond Cedar River Park and the Hippodrome. Waterloo had at least one backyard rink just a few blocks from the Playground Commission's enterprise, at the eastside home of George Watson. A goalie during the very first season of Legion hockey in 1927, Watson had passed on his enthusiasm for the game to his son, George, Jr. Of the younger Watson, a nine-year-old defenseman, the *Courier* related he "...has been skating since he was first able to hold his balance, and now he is rated the best of Waterloo's youngest skaters." George Watson Jr. was one of the dozens of players, young and older, who were playing the winter game which had caught on so quickly.

The chance to see a spirited "professional" hockey game brought onlookers from at least as far as Eldora and Arlington, approximately 50 miles to the southwest and northeast of Waterloo respectively. However, regardless of where their trips began, only 1,400 people made it to the Hippodrome on the first Friday of 1929. They watched as Waterloo rolled past the Armour Packers of St. Paul, 6-3. After falling behind 2-1 nearly six minutes into the second period, the Hawks scored the next five goals. Ralph Gorr and Steve Mickey each found the net twice, with Gorr's goals both coming less than a minute apart, first tying the contest, then giving Waterloo the lead for the first time.

A week later, attendance was even worse as St. Mary's College visited the Cattle Congress rink. Below-zero temperatures limited the Legion to just 872 tickets sold. If Waterloo was shorthanded in fan support, St. Mary's was hamstrung by a lineup which included only eight players. Still, Tony Prelesnik scored the only goal of the first period to provide the visitors with a 1-0 lead at intermission. The game turned in the second on Waterloo tallies by Brock

Richardson, Mickey, and Bill Hunter. The locals held off the outmanned St. Mary's team during a scoreless third period to claim a 3-1 victory.

However, frustration was beginning to become evident among Legion hockey officials regarding the team's business fortunes.

"With a large [financial] loss booked up for the night's work," the *Courier* noted in its game summary the next afternoon, "the Legionnaires today were threatening to postpone further hockey games until the flowers bloom again."

Cold weather was a problem. The worst flu season since the epidemic of 1918/19 was also cited as a factor for poor performance at the admission gates. However, the hockey committee was working hard to generate attendance, too. General admission tickets had been reduced back to 50 cents, with kids able to get into the games for 25 cents. During the week, seats could still be purchased from several downtown retailers. Game start times were adjusted to avoid interference with significant high school basketball games. Although it was impossible to offer a season ticket when there was no guarantee how many games would be played, the Legion introduced a $5 ticket pack, containing a dozen vouchers which could be redeemed for any game at the Hippodrome.

Some fans still went beyond attending the games in support of the squad. A Mr. T.M. Buchanan provided the club with wool blankets for the reserves to sit under while they were on the bench.

"After the boys have played and become warm, there is too much danger of taking cold with only a sweater about them," Buchanan explained.

The Legion Team

A better crowd did turn out on Friday, January 18th to see the visiting Chicago Athletic Association. After playing a close game in Waterloo the previous January, CAA had improved its hockey squad. The organization had dropped its track and field team to focus more on winter sports, while simultaneously improving its roster with former Chicago Yacht Club and Lake Shore Athletic Club skaters when those hockey teams disbanded. Waterloo also went into the matchup without veteran Brock Richardson who had hurt his foot while working at John Deere.

The Hawks still started quickly with goals in the first seven minutes by Clarence Keyes and Gene Collette. CAA rallied to even the score, but Keyes' second of the night, 3:45 before the end of the first period, gave the Legion a 3-2 lead. Chicago tied the affair with the only goal during the middle period, then Lloyd Victel delivered the winner for the visitors, making the count 4-3 with 9:15 to play. A determined effort to square the score in the closing minutes was denied as Chicago goalie Ed Thompson made 12 saves in the final 20 minutes. Waterloo played without Malcolm for part of the contest after he was clipped with a stick near his right eye.

The best attendance of the season to that point, reported at 2,800, made the Friday night matchup more fun for everyone involved. Many of the fans on hand took the ice themselves for skating races at intermission. Some may have also come home with an amusing story reported in the newspaper the next day:

> Few persons that noted the wild waving of a revolver last night by Gerald (Jerry) Holton, timekeeper of the Waterloo Legion and Chicago Athletic Association game, realized the

near catastrophe that loomed before the timekeeper's vision if a goal had been made in the last 30 seconds of the second period.

Jerry found himself in the most embarrassing position possible to a timekeeper during a close game when his gun jammed and he couldn't make himself heard because of the yells of the crowd.

At the end of the second period, Jerry confidently held up his gun with much dignity to announce the close of the period. But the cylinder jammed and the gun wouldn't fire.

Realizing that if a goal were made before he could stop the game, he'd probably be chased from the building, Jerry howled his hardest. But it was hopeless.

Finally, he turned to Emil Steffen, detective, who was sitting near, and besought aid. After discarding, out of respect for the Hippodrome roof, the idea of firing his own revolver, Steffen grabbed the defective pistol, wrenched the cylinder clear, and fired the gun.

Legion shooting would need to be much more accurate against their next opponent, the infantry men from Fort Snelling.

* * *

In the early 1800's, Fort Snelling was established as a frontier outpost nearly 40 years before the territory it protected became the State of Minnesota. The Twin Cities of St. Paul and Minneapolis grew up around the fort, located at the confluence of the Mississippi and Minnesota Rivers. Soldiers stationed there would campaign against Native American tribes throughout the northern Great Plains and help preserve the Union during the Civil War. The U.S. Third Infantry was first based at Fort Snelling in 1888. After being deployed and posted in various locations before The

World War, the unit returned to its Minnesota home in 1921. A somewhat leisurely postwar environment, including a variety of recreational opportunities, led to Fort Snelling being nicknamed "The Country Club of the Army," and for the Third Infantry, that meant the opportunity to play hockey in the winter.

In the late 1920's, Fort Snelling had an officer in charge of overseeing athletics. Capt. S.F. Howard managed a schedule of hockey games against college and semiprofessional opponents and had helped arrange the first trip by a Third Infantry team to Waterloo the previous January. When the soldiers returned in early 1929, their lineup included a notable addition. Lt. Tito Moscatelli had been raised in Minnesota's Iron Range before becoming a cadet at the United States Military Academy. While attending West Point, Moscatelli served as captain of Army's varsity team for a season. His military career would eventually take him to a much higher rank, when he earned a colonel's eagle.

While Fort Snelling had added Lt. Moscatelli, they had lost Sgt. Steve Mickey, who had scored two of the soldier's four goals against Waterloo in the first 1928 matchup. The left-handed forward was given a three month furlough and came to the Cedar Valley with his wife when an opportunity to play for the Becker-Chapman Post and work for John Deere became available. Born in Duluth in 1902, Mickey's family moved to Alabama early in his childhood. He did not take up hockey until later in his adolescence after returning north. Mickey also was a quarterback on the football field for service teams. On the ice during the five years he was stationed at Fort Snelling, Mickey occasionally played with other semiprofessional and industrial league teams as well, including the South St. Paul Cowboys.

The Legion and the soldiers were scheduled to meet on Friday, January 25th. However, snowy winter weather delayed the matchup one night due to Fort Snelling's travel difficulties. When the teams did get to the Hippodrome Saturday, the offense arrived late. The matchup was scoreless until the 17-minute mark of the second period, when Moscatelli fired a shot into the net past Jack Hand. It took Waterloo the remainder of the second and most of the third before answering, as Ralph Gorr and Cameron MacKinnon moved the puck to Bob Collette who zipped into the offensive zone for the equalizer with 7:10 remaining. Waterloo continued to maintain pressure, but the game remained 1-1 into the final minute of play until Clarence Keyes fired a low shot into the net for the dramatic winning goal. The game account noted that it was "...fine hockey and gave the fair sized crowd which turned out to witness the postponed game several thrills..."

At Becker-Chapman headquarters, sports proponents were hoping for another successful late comeback near the end of January. The Iowa Legion's boxing bill had not been prepared properly as of January 23rd, according to a *Courier* report. Time was running out to get something to the State House of Representatives for consideration during its brief annual session. Part of the difficulty may have been the failure of other Legion-backed efforts to legalize the sport earlier in the decade. Another problem was the willingness of boxing promoters and fans in many communities to stage illegal fights, flouting the formal prohibitions against the bouts. With time becoming critical, the organization's legislative committee found traction and was able to compile the necessary elements to have a proposal for the General

Assembly's Judicial Committee within a week.

Locally, the closing days of January brought another anticipated announcement from Waterloo's Legion hockey committee; for the second consecutive year, arrangements had been completed to bring a Canadian opponent to the Cedar Valley. Speculation had focused on the Winnipeg-based Elmwood Millionaires, but ultimately a different Winnipeg club was secured, the Maple Leafs. With the publicity of the series came related news of an increase in hockey ticket prices. General admission would increase to 75 cents. Roy Malcolm described the need for a change in policy with a statement similar to the post's explanation under similar circumstances in 1928, saying, "The Canadian team is coming here at great expense to us, but their coming is in keeping with the Legion's policy of providing Waterloo hockey fans with the finest competition possible."

The increase took effect for the final game before Winnipeg visited. Waterloo slated a tune-up on February 1st against the Chicago College of Osteopathy. Advertisements for the matchup labeling the visitors the "Bone-Crushers" might have given the impression that the game would be fiercely fought. However, the 1,200 in attendance saw the most lopsided Legion victory of the winter.

Just one minute after the opening faceoff, Mickey scored to start the onslaught. Less than another minute passed before it was 2-0 on a goal by Bob Collette. The visitors did chalk a tally onto the scoreboard before the game was four minutes old, but a surge just prior to intermission mirrored the quick start, and Waterloo owned a 4-1 cushion after 20 minutes. They added three more in the second and two in the third for a 9-1 final. Mickey finished the contest with three goals and Keyes with two. The Hawks limited the

College of Osteopathy to just a dozen shots, while putting 27 of their own on net. With the easy win, Waterloo was 5-2 for the season.

* * *

"THE WAR IS ON…Canada Will Invade Iowa With the Strongest Hockey Team That the Dominion Ever Sent Into the State. *Every Patriotic Iowan Should Enlist in the Army of Rooters at the Hockey Games!*" blared a newspaper ad on the day before the Legion's first game versus the Winnipeg Maple Leafs. It went on to dub the visitors, "…one of the fastest organizations north of the Canadian border."

The Maple Leafs were collected from a number of different teams in Winnipeg. Little else can be definitively said about them. Even the players' first names were left unrecorded in newspaper coverage and are now lost. Whatever their origins and later exploits, the Leafs agreed to come to Waterloo for a pair of games on Wednesday, February 6th and Friday, February 8th. The winner of the series would be determined by the total number of goals scored in both games, a format which had been used early in Stanley Cup history and other playoff situations. The rationale for using aggregate scoring was that it would encourage both teams to continue playing hard, even if one side managed to take a large lead in either game.

As they had a year earlier, Waterloo took advantage of Winnipeg's travel fatigue in the first game. Less than five minutes into the matchup, Clarence Keyes found Steve Mickey for the opening score. The Legion players could not make it 2-0 before intermission despite a five minute Winnipeg penalty after a player threw his stick at the puck, but early in the second period, Keyes settled the disk and knocked in a quick shot to build the lead. Waterloo maintained the two-goal edge until nine minutes remained in regulation, when a Maple Leaf defenseman named Clark sent a whistling chance into the net from long distance. Jack Hand was able to stop the other six shots he saw in the period and made 28 saves during the 2-1 victory. His counterpart, a big netminder listed only as Kellogg, was lauded for a fine effort with 25 saves. The largest crowd of the season, estimated at 3,500, turned out for the game.

One of the most distinctive figures on the ice during the matchup was not a player for either team. Referee Frank Pennas had officiated a few games in Waterloo, and according to the *Courier*'s account, "...he is firm in his decisions and the boys respect him because they know he knows his stuff." The St. Paul native patrolled the ice during American Hockey Association games in the winter and called balls and strikes during the summer for professional baseball leagues in the Midwest and Southeast. He would have been easily recognizable from bleachers well removed from either the diamond or ice; Pennas had only one arm as the result of an accident involving a train when he was a teenager.

The referee and both teams returned the Hippodrome for the Friday rematch, which began better for the visitors. With a little less than seven minutes remaining before the first intermission, a well-executed play by the Maple Leafs led to a tap-in goal for their center, Inkster. Waterloo tied the game 20 seconds into the second, the result of a Keyes shot and Mickey assist. A mishandled puck by Kellogg, knocked over his own goal line with under three minutes to go in the second period, pushed the Legion ahead 2-1. Reportedly, Kellogg looked back at goal judge Fred Wagner after the play and shrugged off the go-ahead score, saying, "Well, I'm just big hearted, that's all."

In the final period, the Leafs justified Kellogg's calm and confidence, holding Waterloo to just four shots on goal. Clark tied the game at 6:10, then Inkster notched his second of the night, the winner, eight minutes later. After Roy Malcolm was knocked into the boards and left the contest with a knee injury, two more Winnipeg goals with under two minutes remaining stretched the margin, leading to a 5-2 final. Those scores also gave the Maple Leafs the edge in total goals for the series, 6-4.

While they could have steamed back to Winnipeg, the Maple Leafs agreed to stay in Waterloo for a third game, just as the Buffaloes had done a year earlier. With two days to recover from his spill, Malcolm was back in the lineup as a reserve. He probably had not stepped onto the ice before Winnipeg took the lead 80 seconds into the game. That goal stood as the only scoring until the early third period when the Maple Leafs padded their advantage. Trailing 2-0 despite an edge in chances, the Legion finally broke through at 14:25 when Bob Collette lifted a shot to the back of the net. Winnipeg would hold on for a 2-1 victory, but the teams had perhaps seen enough of each other, and frustration eventually boiled over when Collette dropped the gloves for a scrap with his counterpart Clark. Fans may also have been worn out by the time the Monday matchup was played; attendance was reportedly unimpressive for the final game of the series.

By February 1929, attitudes were beginning to change about how Legion hockey could be sustained in the Cedar Valley. A *Courier* report indicated that Becker-Chapman leaders were lobbying other Iowa communities and Legion posts to consider forming a league with at least four teams. The Cedar Rapids Legion had been given specifics about investing in a team and facility, while Fort Dodge officials had apparently come to Waterloo for a firsthand look at hockey in the Hippodrome. Des Moines, Davenport, and Dubuque were also each mentioned as possible destinations on the circuit. The story continued:

> Formation of an Iowa hockey league would be a great aid to Waterloo and every city interested in the plan. Interest would be more keen and attendance greater, local legion officials admit, if Waterloo's opponents came from cities which are Waterloo's natural rivals, commercially and otherwise.
>
> The hockey league plan will be pushed throughout the summer months...
>
> (*Waterloo Courier*, February 12, 1929)

With a few weeks of cold weather remaining, Becker-Chapman players knew they would have a few more opportunities to improve on a record which stood at 6-4. A February 15th game against Fort Snelling on the Friday after the Winnipeg series was postponed to give players and spectators both an opportunity to recover from the games against the Maple Leafs. For post officials who may have been thinking about organizing a league, the more immediate task was to make sure the remainder of their 1928/29 ice time was profitable.

* * *

Waterloo natives were enjoying the last part of winter in sporting fashion during late February and early March, 1929. The playground commission's industrial league games continued. On the last Saturday in February, a collection of Waterloo's top amateurs organized themselves for a 90-mile trip to Dubuque and a contest against that community's hockey enthusiasts. Waterloo players returned with the laurels from a 2-1 victory. For those who had seen hockey games at the Hippodrome or Cedar River Park but were unsure of their skating ability, broomball became an alternative. Several prominent citizens took the ice on another late winter evening to bat around a basketball as the Lions Club claimed a 4-1 victory against the local Rotarians in a battle of rival civic organizations.

The Legion concluded February with a rivalry game of their own against the Minnesota Mining & Manufacturing squad which had tripped them up when the schedule opened on Christmas Day. The tilt on Wednesday, February 20th, was a thriller, worth the half hour wait after the visitors' late arrival and additional time needed to find skates for at least one opponent who had forgotten to pack them. Waterloo besieged the 3M net with 13 shots in the first period, pulling ahead midway through the frame on a score by Louis Webber, and building the lead to 2-0 by intermission thanks to Steve Mickey. Just over halfway through the second, Les Munn and Elmer Nelson had erased the margin and tied the score, but a Cameron MacKinnon tally 3:50 before the period was concluded put Waterloo back in front.

It appeared that 3M might frustrate the Becker-Chapman side for a second time. After retying the score, the guests pulled ahead with only 7:40 remaining in the game when Bill Parker's shot beat Jack Hand. The clock wound down below 3:00 to play before MacKinnon squared the game with his second of the night. Then with 1:20 to go, Bob Collette delivered a pass to Mickey, which the sergeant knocked in for the decisive point. While Mickey's goal may have settled the contest on the scoreboard at 5-4, "just to be sure that the cash visitors would feel that they had their money's worth...both teams attempted to stage a royal battle in front of the press box near the end of the third period. It looked like a cat and dog fight for a while," the *Courier* sports page reported. Not surprisingly, Collette was one of the principle participants in the fracas.

Moving into March, fighting on the canvas rather than the ice returned to focus. One hundred members of the Walnut Street Baptist Church prepared a statement reflecting their opposition to the Legion boxing bill and forwarded it to Black Hawk County legislators as the General Assembly prepared to consider the measure. The House Judicial Committee had passed the proposal to the full chamber for its consideration on March 13th. After representatives spent much of the day arguing the issue, the result was an unequivocal knockout as 68 of the 103 voting members, including legislators from Waterloo and Cedar Falls, were against the measure. Party affiliation made little difference in the result. With the House dominated by a Republican supermajority, GOP legislators cast the bulk of votes on both sides of the issue.

"So long as [boxing] is not legal in the eyes of the law," the *Courier* opined the next day, "it will not be popular. The chance involved in attending a fight show in this state is too great a risk for the entertainment provided."

During the weekend prior to the boxing vote, hockey season at the Hippodrome had come to an end. Becker-Chapman leaders spoke plainly about the need for the finale to be a success from a business standpoint, leading the *Courier* to explain, that "Whether or not Waterloo is going to remain the hockey center of Iowa depends to a great extent on the response made by fans tomorrow evening..." Whether it was a result of that implication – that the future of hockey in the community was at stake – or the practical fact that the Cattle Congress ice would thaw and the season would soon end with the arrival of warmer spring weather, 2,000 advance tickets for the matchup against Fort Snelling had been sold by the morning of the March 8th contest.

The teams squared off at 8:30 p.m. in front of 3,000 people. The first period was wild; the soldiers' Angus Johnson scored the first goal 8:40 into the game, but the Legion responded with three-in-a-row from Roy Malcolm, Clarence Keyes, and Brock Richardson. Adding another Fort Snelling marker just before intermission, five of the 15 total shots on goal during the opening 20 minutes found the net. The Legion took over in the second period, with Richardson and Keyes each recording their second goals of the evening, plus an additional score by Bill Hunter. Waterloo and Fort Snelling split the final period with two goals apiece, including Keyes' third of the game, for an 8-4 victory. The win gave the Legion a season-ending record of 8-4.

Financially, the game against Fort Snelling was not enough to bring Waterloo hockey to ".500" for the season. The dozen hockey games, plus other skating activities at the Hippodrome had generated $12,000. Becker-Chapman ice-related expenses during the winter of 1928/29 totaled $13,600. Although the effort had not yielded the profits of the previous two years, the prevailing feeling was that games should continue when the weather cooled again the following December.

"The Legion looks upon hockey as one of its services to the community," explained a newspaper editorial after the Fort Snelling game, "and not as a money-making proposition."

That noble sentiment would be tested under the harshest of economic conditions in the coming year, as the Legion – like every other organization, business, and family – dealt with the tribulations of The Great Depression.

PESSIMISM NOT INTENDED

In 1929, the Becker-Chapman Legion Post was kept busy helping former service men in need. The post found jobs for at least 300 veterans as The Great Depression began to affect the country. Hundreds of dollars were spent aiding soldiers and their families dealing with financial strains. Becker-Chapman officials also interceded to help secure money from Iowa and Black Hawk County veteran relief funds. Meeting the practical needs of those who fought in The World War would continue to occupy the post in subsequent years. "During the months of business depression," Commander Charles McKinstry reported in late 1930, "special attention was given to the unemployment problem...The three largest industrial plants in Waterloo gave preference to veterans who were recommended through our adjutant's office."

Just after the 1928/29 hockey season had ended, Legion members turned their attention to organizing the effort to avert disaster as spring rain and thawing snow flooded the Cedar Valley. "For three days," according to the *Courier*, "the former soldiers battled, with other citizens, day and night against the rising tide, building dikes and rescuing families from submerged homes." As the year continued, the post and its more than 900 members overcame the financial losses from the previous winter's effort at the Hippodrome rink through various fundraising projects. There was no question hockey would return in the waning days of the calendar year.

However, preparations for the new season did not include scheduling games in an all-Iowa hockey circuit. The league project, considered in early 1929, never found traction in other communities. Economic uncertainties caused by the early months of The Great Depression may have had some effect. More immediate concerns like a lack of hockey facilities and the challenge of creating an interested fanbase could have been even more daunting for prospective hockey promoters. Even in the Cattle Congress Hippodrome, it would have been difficult to have played a predetermined league schedule without the assurance that the ice would not thaw during warm spells. The keenest supporters of the game in Waterloo – where the sport had already been successful – did not even have the backing to add the necessary infrastructure for artificial ice.

The future of eastern Iowa's already well-established Mississippi Valley Baseball League was even in jeopardy during the winter of 1929/30. Teams in Rock Island and Moline, Illinois, each reportedly struggled through the 1929 schedule on the eight-team loop. Waterloo also finished the year at a deficit after having had trouble filling the ballpark. "What action the Hawk officials will take in an effort to start the [1930] season all even is a matter of conjecture, but a blanket selling campaign and a dance in February..." were among the fundraising concepts which came to the attention of Waterloo sportswriters.

The biggest problem for the Mississippi Valley League was the result of an impropriety of the kind so often uncovered during the aftermath of a financial crisis. George Huckins had purchased the Cedar Rapids Bunnies baseball club before the 1929 season and, according to the *Courier*, "...ran the club in major league style, outfitting his boys in the best and providing them plenty of spending money." He and his father, Elmer, convinced several local investors to buy into a business plan which would purchase factory overstock cigars at a deep discount before reselling them at retail prices for a huge profit. Those backers included Bunnies field manager Bill Speas and Dubuque team owner Fred Leiser. In December, Huckins was arrested when he could not pay his bills, and the fraudulent scheme – which had swindled more than two million dollars from its victims over five years without ever buying a single wholesale cigar – was revealed. Convicted and sentenced to seven years in prison for the scam, George Huckins eventually had the verdict overturned but died in jail awaiting a new trial in 1932.

In January 1930, Mississippi Valley owners did decide they would take the field during the upcoming summer. The Bunnies were confiscated from Huckins by the league. Belden Hill, president of the circuit and a Cedar Rapids native, convinced 65 local businesses to contribute $100 each in order to keep the team active. The Hawks, Bunnies, both Illinois teams, plus clubs in Davenport, Dubuque, Burlington, and Keokuk all swung away for 126 games.

Huckins was still a respected citizen of Cedar Rapids when hockey players began appearing in Waterloo and construction on the Cattle Congress rink began. Unlike the previous winter, the Becker-Chapman team retained only a few veterans. Roy Malcolm remained with the club and Clarence Keyes stayed on for a third season. Healthy competition determined the other names on the Waterloo roster. Goalie Jack Hand returned but lost his starting job and spent 1929/30 on the bench. Hand was supplanted by former Chicago Athletic Association netminder Ed Thompson, whose CAA teammate, Lloyd Victel, also came to Waterloo in December looking for a hockey job but left again hoping to make the roster for a team in Houghton, Michigan. Another former Legion opponent who joined the squad was winger Angus Johnson, who had played against Waterloo for Fort Snelling.

New forward Carroll Stuart was noted as a "local" player, although the designation was misleading. Stuart had been raised in Canada before moving to Chicago as a teenager. He came to Waterloo in late 1928 and took a job at Black's department store but did not play for the Legion that winter. As a sportsman, Stuart first gained local notoriety on the golf course by finishing second during the 1929 Iowa State Amateur Tournament. In seven July days, the 21-year-old played over 200 competitive holes in conjunction with the event, culminating with a two-round, 34-hole match play final. Besides his ability with wedges and short irons, Stuart was also recognizable by his flamboyant clothing on the links, according to a contemporary Associated Press report, which noted, he "...appears daily for his round of golf in different attire. Sometimes he changes also between morning and afternoon rounds."

With Malcolm planning to take over as the hockey club's left winger, there was plenty of opportunity at the defensive positions. Waterloo reloaded with Herb Fallis and speedy Joe Johnston who both came to the Cedar Valley from Kansas City, plus Louie Sterba, who had been working and playing hockey in Minneapolis. Buddy Hugar, from Fort William, Ontario, also joined the team for the start of the season. As temperatures dropped well below freezing in mid-December, several others skated at the Hippodrome with hopes of finding a place in the lineup.

One new member of the team did not wear skates. Becker-Chapman leaders hired Jay Henson as the general manager for all of their winter activities on the Cattle Congress grounds. Henson was the post's former vice commander in charge of veterans relief efforts and very active in Waterloo Legion projects. During the closing months of the war, he had served with the small American force deployed to far eastern Siberia, "…which experience should stand him in hand this winter when the old thermometer stands below the zero mark," quipped the *Becker-Chapman Barrage* newsletter. The publisher of Waterloo's *Shoppers Guide* advertising paper and a landlord, Henson was short but had "a sunny disposition," and lived on Waterloo's east side, several blocks east of Cedar River Park.

Assisted by a small advisory committee which included some of the post's top men, Henson changed several hockey policies. First, he eliminated reserved tickets at the Hippodrome, other than $1 box seats, and cut general admission back to 50 cents. Admission for children was reduced to 10 cents. Next, he planned to schedule as many games as possible on holiday and Sunday afternoons, rather than Friday nights as in prior seasons, with the hope of drawing better attendance. Henson did not tinker with Roy

Malcolm's status as team leader on the ice, and named the veteran the club's captain as initial practices were getting under way.

W.B. Forshay Company was slated to be the first opponent of the winter on Christmas Day, but was scratched less than a week prior to the matchup. Instead, the 3M team came to Waterloo as the opening day challenger for a second consecutive year. A large crowd was on hand for the game, but the exact attendance is uncertain. The *Courier* set the number at 2,500, while the Legion figure was around 1,500.

Whatever the count, those at the rink saw another close game between Waterloo and Minnesota Mining and Manufacturing. Just over a minute into the game, Keyes set up Malcolm at his new forward position for the first goal of the afternoon. Waterloo remained ahead 1-0 through intermission. In the second, 3M's Elmer Nelson continued to cause trouble for the Legion side, as he had the previous year; after setting up the tying goal, he dashed to the net for a go-ahead score at 16:30. Four minutes into the third, a blast by Fallis made the game 2-2. However, with under three minutes remaining, a shot by Nelson ricocheted off the leg of a Waterloo skater, past Thompson, and into the net for the winning goal.

Despite the loss, the *Barrage* gave a glowing review of the logistical aspects of the effort: "Many comments were heard complimenting Henson on his executive ability, for there was no doubt that this first game was handled far better than in any previous years…The Legionnaires on the various jobs did themselves proud. In fact this game will go down in history as a success." As for the players, they would have the opportunity for their first official success a week later.

* * *

After scoring a goal during his first game in Waterloo, Herb Fallis – occasionally referred to by his middle name, Elmer – really began to build a reputation on New Year's Day. The big defenseman stood six feet tall and could let go a booming shot. Born in southwestern Manitoba in late 1905, Fallis had been in the United States nearly a year before coming to northeast Iowa, making his way first to Kansas City. He would be a versatile player for the Becker-Chapman Post, although his competitive zeal may have occasionally irritated some of the squad's more savvy players. Holding a large lead in a game later in the 1929/30 season, the team reportedly decided at the second intermission not to run up the score during the third period so fans would not be dissuaded from attending a rematch later in the weekend. Apparently abandoning the plan, Fallis scored three goals himself in the final 20 minutes that evening.

"'I didn't try to make those goals,' explained Fallis when questioned by his mates. 'They simply went in,'" he said, according to the *Courier*'s account of the incident.

At least some of the other players were apparently skeptical of his version of events.

However, on New Year's Day, the Legion needed all of the scoring Fallis could provide. Contending with unseasonably warm weather and soft ice while facing Wisconsin's Janesville Independents, Waterloo went ahead 3:30 into the second period when Fallis clubbed a shot into the net. Not quite four minutes later, the visitors tied the score, but at the nine minute mark of the period, Fallis whistled the puck to the goal from center ice past a screened and startled opposing netminder. When that score stood up to give Waterloo a 2-1 victory, the *Courier* correspondent on hand dubbed the blue-liner "Dead-Eye Fallis" and remarked, "Fallis is a defenseman but that does not mean he has to hang out around the goal. He simply delights in taking an occasional sortie up the ice and he is right handy with stick and skates."

Four days later, the team returned to the rink for the first Sunday contest of the winter, joined by a crowd of 1,200. Frank Pennas, who had refereed several games at the Hippodrome the previous season, was on hand but serving as the coach of an opponent sponsored by a Minneapolis paper distributor. The Van Paper club, known as the VanGuards, included Herb Brooks Sr., whose namesake son would become one of the most well-known figures in U.S. hockey 50 years later upon leading the nation to Olympic gold versus the Soviet Union. A number of other players from the Twin Cities who skated for various area teams were also on the VanGuard roster, including goalie Earl Franz, familiar in Waterloo after coming to town less than two weeks earlier with 3M. The following winter, Franz would join the St. Paul Saints of the minor Central Hockey League.

The Legion got to Franz for a goal just 1:10 into the game as Fallis fed a pass for Clarence Keyes to finish from close range. Franz stopped the other 14 chances Waterloo sent his way for the remainder of the afternoon. At the opposite end of the rink, Elmer Nelson, another 3M regular, tied the score at the two minute mark. The visitors went ahead five minutes into the period and closed the day's scoring at 8:20. The 3-1 tally held from that point through the end of the contest, which became increasingly heated but never boiled over into fisticuffs.

Although the Becker-Chapman squad lost the game, the team found a new defenseman in the process. Gordon "Doc" Brown had wanted to join Waterloo for the 1928/29 season, but there was no place for him on the roster. The sturdy defenseman had first visited the Cattle Congress grounds as a member of the St. Paul Hook 'em Cows in 1927 and returned on a regular basis after that with several other clubs from Minneapolis and St. Paul. After joining Waterloo formally in the week after the Van Paper game, Brown became the team's largest player and gave Roy Malcolm the opportunity to move Fallis from defense to center. Neither Brown, nor the recently returned Lloyd Victel, had much time to practice with the team before a January 12th tilt with St. Mary's College.

When the Redmen from the small school in Winona, Minnesota, had visited Waterloo the year before, the college's hockey club was just getting reorganized. According to the account of that initial meeting, two of the St. Mary's players, "...had never seen a hockey game before. The St. Mary's team did have a veteran line of six men who have played a lot of hockey outside of college. When those men tired, there were no other red-sweatered hosts to throw into competition." Despite their limited experience, St. Mary's did not lose many other games in 1928/29. In the years that followed, the school would develop one of the top college squads in the western United States, traveling regularly during Christmas breaks to meet eastern teams including Yale, Harvard, Princeton, and Brown and skating in the country's best hockey venues like Boston Garden and New York's Madison Square Garden. After a handful of exciting seasons, the program disbanded as many of its star players graduated and the broader pool of students at the school dwindled during economic hard times.

A key 1929/30 St. Mary's addition who Waterloo had not seen the previous year was goaltender Oscar Almquist. Like much of the college team, the 21-year-old freshman had come south to Winona from Minnesota's Iron Range, the hockey nursery of the United States in that era. He played on nearly every team St. Mary's fielded, including football, basketball, baseball, and track. After graduating as an All-American, he returned north to play minor league professional hockey in Eveleth and St. Paul before becoming a longtime high school coach and principal in Roseau, Minnesota. Almquist's long, successful tenure there helped him earn induction into the United States Hockey Hall of Fame.

Few other changes to the Redmen's roster were necessary. Brother combinations Tony and Louis Prelesnik and Chester and Charles Eldridge remained intact. Like Almquist, Tony Prelesnik would later be recognized with All-American hockey honors and also starred on the St. Mary's football team. Eddie Lynch was another football player during autumns in Winona. Defenseman Matt Lahti rounded out the lineup and served as the school's hockey captain.

Although the feeling among Becker-Chapman leaders was that, "this St. Mary's aggregation is a bunch of dandy nice fellows..." the January 12th game was rough, highlighted by a high stick which knocked out Keyes at one point and resulted in an almost unheard of five minute penalty to Tony Prelesnik. Despite being handled roughly, Keyes scored two goals during the matchup, as did Fallis in the 4-3 Waterloo victory. Both of the Eldridge brothers tallied for the visitors, whose first score had come from

Louis Prelesnik, tying the game at 1-1 in the first period. Ed Thompson was arguably the day's biggest star, making 26 saves and outdueling Almquist for the win.

Local hockey fans would see much more of the Redmen, but before they returned to oppose the Legion late in the month, a collection of players known as the Minnesota Wanderers visited for a game on bitterly cold and windy January 19th. The group was led by lawyer, adventurer, and Yale alumnus Alfred Lindley, who had played college hockey for the Bulldogs but went to the Olympics, both summer and winter, as a rower and skier respectively. The visiting lineup also included two of the Hanson brothers – Oscar and either Joe or Julius – whose Augsburg College team had been denied the chance to play in the 1928 Olympics. Minneapolis notables and future minor leaguers Ted Breckheimer and Leo Schatzlein also made the trip.

Keyes and Schatzlein each scored in the opening period. The pace picked up dramatically in the early second. Breckheimer nudged the Wanderers ahead sixty seconds after the game restarted, but less than a minute later, Fallis tied it again for Waterloo. Carroll Stuart gave the locals the lead permanently at 2:45, and on the ensuing shift, Fallis scored again. The Legion held their 4-2 cushion until a pair of late scores brought the final total to 6-2.

The post planned to expand from the Sunday schedule for a pair of games during the last full weekend in January; the Friday and Sunday matchups were intended to be the team's annual international series, with a new Canadian opponent, the Weyburn Beavers of the Southern Saskatchewan Senior Hockey League. However, the Beavers canceled their road trip several days before they were slated to depart. Waterloo attendance had been lagging, with typical crowds between

1,000 and 1,500, and while a team from north of the border may have generated additional interest, the added expense also created a potential for greater financial losses. St. Mary's was quickly contacted to serve as a stand-in for the weekend.

Even with a substitute opponent, and without Keyes who had injured his hip against the Wanderers, the series yielded two of the best-played games of the Legion hockey era, led by Thompson and Almquist. The *Courier* praised both after a 1-1 tie Friday, saying of Thompson:

> He dove, he sprawled – bounced them from his chest and singled with his broad-bladed stick when a strike would have been in and not out. They ganged and framed on him, but he was impenetrable…[Almquist] was also a marvel. The tighter the corner he was placed in, the harder he fought. With utter disregard to his physical well being, he would plunge full length on the ice and smother the pellet with some 180 pounds of brawn.

Louis Prelesnik finally scored six minutes into the third period on a long chance which dipped and skipped off of the ice, trickling through Thompson's pads. At 8:30, Brown got the goal back, finding a loose puck at close range and blasting a shot into the St. Mary's net. Still square at the end of regulation, a pair of five minute overtime periods could not change the score. When it was over, the paper's enthusiastic reporter told his readers to prepare for "the hockey game of the century" in the Sunday rematch.

The goaltenders, especially Thompson, were still in top form when the teams got back together. In the opening period, the Waterloo netminder made 13 saves to keep the game scoreless. That allowed Stuart to record the first goal early in the second, taking a feed from Brown and putting the puck quickly behind Almquist. Before the second intermission, the game swung the other way; Louis Prelesnik navigated to the front of the net to knock in the equalizer, then assisted on a go-ahead tally by Lahti.

After St. Mary's had carried the play through 40 minutes, Waterloo roared back in the third. Consistent pressure led to a series of penalties on the Redmen, and at one point they were left with just two defenders and their goaltender on the ice. That's when Victel pulled the puck from a scrum in the goalmouth and slammed a chance into the net with 6:25 remaining. As before, neither team could convert a chance during ten minutes of overtime, and the final remained 2-2. The largest crowd of the season to that point, between just 1,600 and 1,900, was on hand for a matchup which the often-hyperbolic *Courier* seems to have appropriately labeled, "epic."

* * *

After suffering a dislocated hip and a bad cold, which together had put him in the hospital, it was turning out to be a painful winter for Clarence Keyes. He attempted to return for the second St. Mary's tie on January 26th, but aggravated the hip injury and could not complete the game. Despite his slight build, the 5-foot, 5-inch forward and former team captain was tremendously swift and shifty on his skates. The *Courier* praised him during his absence, "...as probably the best of all those who have ever demonstrated their stuff on the Hippodrome ice...barring further injuries to his small frame work, [he] should find a place in professional hockey next season."

Unfortunately, Keyes' age made him an unlikely candidate for advancement to a higher level of the sport. He had been born in southern Ontario in 1895, the same year as Fred Becker, Carl Chapman, and Roy Malcolm. Like those others, he went to Europe to serve in the World War, taking his oath to King George V and joining the Canadian Expeditionary Force as a member of the Niagara Rangers Battalion in early 1917. The unit was transported to England and later France, where blue-eyed, brown-haired, 21-year-old Keyes served as a lance corporal.

After the fighting ended, Keyes returned to Canada and migrated west. By 1923, he arrived in Drinkwater, Saskatchewan, a small town southeast of Moose Jaw, along a branch of the Soo Line Railroad which ran to Minot, North Dakota and points south. Keyes took farm jobs and worked for a local hardware business. In the winter, he played hockey, helping the Drinkwater team reach the provincial finals in 1927. After that success, Keyes spent one final summer in Saskatchewan, then moved to Waterloo at age 32 to become a starter on the Becker-Chapman hockey squad and a shift worker at John Deere.

Waterloo did not need the 34-year-old Keyes in the lineup to easily improve their record to 4-2-2 on January 31st. "Ping" Hill, former teammate of Ed Thompson and Lloyd Victel with the Chicago Athletic Association, helped fill the void against an opponent from the Windy City. The visiting club came from the north side neighborhood of Rogers Park, situated on Lake Michigan between Loyola and Northwestern Universities. With a perfect record in the Chicago Amateur League, Rogers Park had reportedly not even been scored against in six games, but the Becker-

Chapman side changed that trend with a customary early goal in the first matchup of another Friday-Sunday series.

Just over five minutes into the opening period, Herb Fallis pushed a puck over the goal line. Carroll Stuart then fired a shot into the net to build the lead ten minutes later. In the second, Gordon Brown and Hill doubled the advantage, before Rogers Park tallied twice in less than a minute. However, another goal by Stuart with 40 seconds remaining before intermission completed the scoring for the evening. The Legion limited Rogers Park to just 14 shots in the 5-2 win, less than the 16 they had sent toward the opposing net in the opening period alone.

The visitors had a couple of reasons for optimism before the Sunday rematch. First, the game was to be played under amateur rules which would limit some of the passing plays that had helped the Waterloo offense. Second, reinforcement was scheduled to arrive as Rogers Park captain Harry Vick made his way to the Cedar Valley after missing the Friday tilt. Neither alteration made any difference with Keyes back at the rink; he and Fallis each set the other up for first period goals and the Legion dashed to a 4-0 lead in less than 20 minutes. The tandem finished the matchup with two goals apiece in a 7-1 rout.

Special promotions were announced for the next two-game weekend, as the post tried to build attendance. Local boy scouts were offered free tickets to the Friday tilt. Adult tickets were sold on a buy-one-get-one-free basis. Disappointing crowds had led the *Becker-Chapman Barrage* to even chide its own membership for not attending regularly, saying, "If only every Legionnaire were present at each game, we would have crowds just about double the present number, and although pessimism is not intended, we are confronted with the necessity of getting more people to the games if this sport is to be maintained on the present basis."

The biggest audience of the season – 2,000 people – did arrive for the Friday game on February 7th against a Northern Pacific Railway team, which had been playing throughout the Twin Cities. The visitors included John "Swede" Gustafson, formerly a skater at the University of Minnesota, and defenseman Wally Faust who had played in the American Amateur Hockey Association. Most notable for the local fans was Louis Webber, who had returned to White Bear Lake after the 1928/29 campaign in Waterloo. The former forward skated as a defenseman for the railroad squad.

The *Barrage* summed up the series aptly, noting that the visitors were, "...unable to 'deliver the goods' as per schedule and as per advance notices." Another four-goal first period in the first meeting gave the Legion its second straight runaway win, by an eventual final of 9-1. Fallis led Waterloo with three goals, and all six forwards who played scored at least once. The lopsided opener limited attendance to 1,000 for Waterloo's 5-2 Sunday victory in the rematch. Webber assisted on both Northern Pacific goals, but the final score was closer than much of the contest; the second railroad marker was notched with only five seconds left in regulation. Angus Johnson assisted on a couple of Waterloo tallies and scored another of his own.

Expecting a financial loss for the winter, Jay Henson and the Becker-Chapman hockey leaders decided to bring the season to a close earlier than ever before. The now-familiar St. Mary's Redmen were engaged for one last Friday-Sunday set on February 14th and 16th. Entering the final weekend of the campaign, Waterloo had been generally sailing through an eight-game unbeaten streak. However, the Redmen had consistently played close games against the post. The 900 at the Hippodrome for the penultimate contest saw another matchup of the same ilk.

Thompson was the busier goaltender as the game went to the first intermission scoreless. He made a dozen saves – including one stop on the goal line itself – to nine by St. Mary's Oscar Almquist. The scoreboard still read 0-0 at the second intermission, despite a shot which sailed into the net from Charles Eldridge but was ruled to have entered the cage after the gun sounded to end the period. In the third, Waterloo built pressure on the visitors as Tony Prelesnik, Eldridge, and Louis Prelesnik went to the penalty box in succession, but the Redmen were able to fight through their time shorthanded without yielding a score, although a Becker-Chapman goal was disallowed after Almquist was interfered with. Back at even strength, Keyes finally broke the deadlock with five minutes to go, navigating to the net and depositing an opportunity which counted.

"St. Mary's tried desperately to score during the final minutes," the *Courier* reported, "but the Legion's offense was its best defense, and by keeping the puck in the collegians territory most of the time, a tie goal was averted."

Waterloo's 1-0 Friday win gave the post a 2-0-2 mark versus their prolific opponents from Winona. The Redmen were due for a win in the Sunday finale. Almquist could not be beaten by a clean Becker-Chapman shot, making 31 saves. St. Mary's finally staked him to a lead with under a minute to play in the second period. Tony Prelesnik pounced on a rebound for the go-ahead goal. Back from intermission, Chester Eldridge battled his way to the net and made it 2-0 early in the final period. Waterloo got that goal back when Fallis' shot was deflected in off the stick of defenseman Louis Prelesnik. However, the Legion's opportunity to complete the comeback ended when a penalty put Waterloo shorthanded in the closing minutes. St. Mary's had finally overcome the Legion in the 2-1 decision, ending the home team's head-to-head unbeaten streak and leaving the post with a final record of 8-3-2 in 1929/30.

* * *

In the early winter months of 1928, officials from baseball's American and National Leagues had chosen the American Legion as their partner to renew and grow the warm weather pastime. League presidents and Commissioner Kennesaw Mountain Landis approved $50,000 – equivalent to approximately two-thirds of the salary Babe Ruth had earned from the New York Yankees during the best season of his career the previous summer – to support Legion baseball, which had been sponsored in some areas as early as 1925. It was expected that as many as 100,000 teenagers would sign up to play for local post teams across the United States. The plan included a nationwide playdown, beginning within area Legion districts, then moving to state and regional levels. Starting each July, winning teams would continue to advance all the way to a Legion World Series in early September. It was the beginning of an enduring affiliation between the veterans' organization and the summer sport.

The Becker-Chapman Post was actively involved in baseball immediately in the summer of 1928. Waterloo's team met opponents sponsored by other local Legion organizations in neighboring communities like Cedar Falls and LaPorte City, and as far away as Marshalltown. Not only a community service project, the promotion of the national game was even considered a patriotic act.

"Junior baseball is one of the activities of The American Legion which is meeting with universal cooperation of Legion Posts," the *Becker-Chapman Barrage* reported. "Outfitting a group of youngsters, furnishing them with equipment and competent instruction, is something in the Legion's program which is very much worthwhile, and this activity should be given all the local support possible."

In June 1930, Becker-Chapman leaders appointed Leon Campbell as the post's athletic director. With the assistance of an advisory committee, Campbell was responsible for overseeing all of the local Legion's sporting endeavors, beginning with baseball. He also helped to organize a golf tournament for Becker-Chapman members. The following summer, a rifle team comprised of young sharpshooters was formed and for many decades represented the post at shooting sports competitions.

However, in late October 1930, it was a different committee charged with considering whether hockey would return to Waterloo for a fifth winter. During the 1929/30 season, general admission hockey tickets had generated a total of $7,541.20. Box seats were worth another $1,052, and advertising by local businesses during games netted $440. The total revenues were a little less than $400 short of covering the $9402.23 in rink-related expenses. Roy Malcolm, Jay Henson, Harry Reed, and several others were given the task of determining whether hockey could be profitable again.

In the weeks immediately following the season, there had been considerable optimism. Henson was lauded in the post newsletter, which argued, "Had it not been for Henson and his hockey advisory committee perhaps the loss sustained would have equaled that of last year...The deficit we incurred is a small price to pay for the satisfaction of once again having served the community in which we live."

Six months later, the mood had changed. The early months of the Depression had been difficult on all manner of sporting events and "extraordinary entertainment." Studying conditions surrounding spectator activities, the hockey committee reportedly found "...in most cases, the receipts from the past year had decreased from 10-50%." The resulting recommendation was that hockey should be abandoned. Becker-Chapman members voted to approve the suggestion at the next regular post meeting. The era of Legion hockey in Waterloo was officially over in October 1930.

* * *

The hockey boom of the 1920's brought the sport to new places far more distant from the game's roots than the Cedar Valley. By 1925, a league had been established on artificial ice at rinks around Los Angeles. The California Professional Hockey League would soon expand north to the San Francisco Bay area. The circuit provided its players a remarkable opportunity to skate through a winter season from December to March in a climate much more hospitable than Winnipeg, Manitoba, White Bear Lake, Minnesota, or even Waterloo, Iowa.

In its dealings with the NHL, the California League was recognized with the same status as other minor leagues of the era, and its teams could earn $5,000 if a prospect was purchased. At least half a dozen players advanced from the loop to appear in the National Hockey League. Twice that many stopped in California later in their careers following appearances in the NHL, including Hall of Fame inductees Ernie Johnson and Jack Walker. Many other veterans had top level professional experience in the Pacific Coast Hockey Association and Western Canada Hockey League from the era when those circuits had the opportunity to claim the Stanley Cup and were considered equals to the National Hockey League.

Teams from the Golden State could even hold their own against NHL opposition. Following the 1929/30 season, the Boston Bruins and Chicago Black Hawks visited California for an exhibition tour. The Black Hawks lost at least twice during the trip. The Stanley Cup runner-up Bruins avoided defeat, but opposing forwards Bud Cook and Art Giroux each went on to wear Boston sweaters in subsequent years after making strong impressions while skating for the Oakland Sheiks and San Francisco Tigers respectively.

During that same spring of 1930, Bill Vaughan and Bob Collette were roommates together in the Melrose Hill neighborhood of Los Angeles near Hollywood. The 25-year-old Collette and his 22-year-old buddy shared the $50 monthly rent. Collette worked to help maintain the ice at a local rink. Vaughan appeared in net for the CPHL team sponsored by Richfield Oil Company.

The next winter, Vaughan moved north to join Oakland's new second team, the Checkers. The better-established Sheiks had won the league championship each of the two previous years, and their 1930/31 roster included new forward Earle Willey. Playing at the 4,200 seat Oakland Ice Arena, which had opened just a year earlier, the Sheiks and Checkers proved to be the top teams in California. In April,

Vaughan and Willey faced each other for the CPHL championship.

According to the *Berkeley Daily Gazette*, Vaughan had been vital to pushing the Checkers through a semifinal versus the Los Angeles Millionaires and, "...deserves all the credit in the world for his headwork and beautiful performance at the Checkers' net. Time and again the Southerners swarmed down the ice on top of him shooting a volley of shots at the cage."

However, Vaughan was unable to pull the Checkers through the first game of the championship series, and his former Waterloo teammate Willey scored the opening goal in a 4-3 Sheiks overtime victory. Game Two in the best-of-five series was played a couple of nights later, and the Checkers rebounded for a hard-hitting 4-2 victory which brought opposing fans over the boards and onto the rink at one point to argue a controversial goal call. Vaughan made 36 saves in the decision. The Sheiks pulled ahead in the series again when they claimed the third contest, 3-1. In Game Four, a Willey assist helped lead to the second overtime matchup of the round, and after an extra ten minute period, the contest ended in a 3-3 tie. Even without a winner, Game Four determined the championship; since the Checkers could finish the series with nothing better than an even 2-2-1 record, the fifth game was called off and the title awarded to the Sheiks by virtue of their better position in the regular season standings.

The Checkers did not return for a second season. Vaughan continued to play however, after moving back to Los Angeles. During the 1932/33 campaign, he was reunited with Willey and Collette, who strapped on his skates again, as all three joined the Hollywood Millionaires. After dwindling to just three teams that season, the CPHL would cease to operate at the end of the 1933 playoffs.

Vaughan, Willey, and Collette were not the only former Waterloo players to find their way to California. Herb Fallis arrived in Los Angeles later and played in the Inter-City Hockey League, heir to the CPHL and the new tenant in the L.A. rinks vacated by the defunct circuit. At age 30 in 1935, he became a U.S. citizen, and by 1940 he moved to Oakland and managed a filling station. Clarence Keyes would also make his living by serving west coast motorists. Leaving his position at John Deere in the months after the Legion decided to discontinue hockey, Keyes took a job at a Los Angeles gas station, then opened a chain of auto parts stores, eventually settling north of Sacramento.

Other former Becker-Chapman hockey stars also departed from Waterloo for various destinations and opportunities. Carroll Stuart returned to Canada and had a notable amateur golfing career there in the 1930's. During World War II, he joined the Canadian Air Force and was stationed near Vancouver before reentering civilian life and taking a job as a country club golf professional near Ottawa. Fred Wagner went to Tennessee and raised hunting dogs with some renown. Roy Malcolm applied for United States citizenship while living in Miami in 1944. At the same time, his son Alan – who according to the *Becker-Chapman Barrage*, had once "marked off [the floors] with blue lines" to play hockey inside at the family home on Waterloo's west side – was by then old enough to serve in the U.S. Navy.

Ed Brucher was only on hiatus from his military career when he helped establish the Becker-Chapman hockey team as post adjutant in 1927. After losing an election for the position of post commander, he became more active in the

Iowa Reserve Officers Association, and was eventually chosen as president of that organization in 1932. A year later, he returned to active duty and remained in the Army working as a logistical officer at Fort Leonard Wood in Missouri during World War II. In the postwar years, he was stationed in the Philippines and Tokyo, working in counterintelligence, before retiring as a colonel in 1953.

The Becker-Chapman Post remained busy serving veterans of the First World War and the community at large. In the summer of 1931, Legionnaires led an effort to build a wading pool for children at Gates Park on Waterloo's east side. That spring, they had also hosted a sold out event which brought Adm. Richard Byrd to the Cedar Valley as he toured the nation lecturing about his successful expedition to the South Pole. The speaking engagement helped offset the expenses from Byrd's mission while also generating funds for Waterloo veteran's relief during the Depression. Ultimately, the Becker-Chapman Post and all of the American Legion would expand in scope during the following decades to represent veterans of many generations and conflicts.

As for hockey in Waterloo, players continued to take the ice at Cedar River Park Lagoon and wherever else they could skate when temperatures fell below freezing. By the late 1950's, a Waterloo club calling itself the Black Hawks was playing in the Hawkeye State League. Opposing teams on the ad hoc loop came from at least Humboldt, Fort Dodge, and Des Moines. Like the Becker-Chapman club – nearly forgotten after the passage of so many winters – the enthusiastic local players still depended on favorable weather to hold their games.

During the winter of 1959/60, the Black Hawks refocused on the Hippodrome – which had been completely rebuilt in 1936 – as a possible home for hockey in the community. Team president and player Ed McEnany encouraged residents to petition the city for action which would renovate the facility. At the time, Waterloo rented the building from the Cattle Congress board for a variety of civic activities. The idea gained momentum and was placed on the ballot for a non-binding resident preference vote in late March.

Courier sportswriter Al Ney lobbied for the idea in his column just days before the poll, "Considering what golf courses, swimming pools, baseball fields and other things cost, the indoor ice rink would be a steal because the building for it already exists."

Ney concluded that whether or not the $100,000 project drew a positive response, it was valuable to put the question to a vote and give residents their say.

The election results appeared to kill the project: 4,124 in favor, 6,612 opposed.

Mayor Ed Jochumsen remarked, "It would appear that our people have voted their pocketbooks. This fits the policy of this administration that taxes are too high now and we must find ways to keep up with progress without increases in taxes."

On the same ballots, residents had also expressed their preference nearly two-to-one not to put fluoride in city water. An even larger ratio was against adopting daylight-saving time. Ultimately, all the results were ignored, to the relief of more progressively-minded citizens.

Cattle Congress officials began a new round of Hippodrome modernizations in the summer of 1961, and ice equipment was considered as the project continued. A year later during a special session, the Waterloo City Council approved an amended 20-year lease for the Hippodrome and nearly $120,000 for all the pieces necessary to make the building a modern ice rink in the winter. Within six weeks, 44,000 feet of pipe had been laid to carry coolant under a newly-poured concrete floor. The quick pace of construction meant that skaters would return to the old barn before 1962 ended. Unlike the Hippodrome of the 1920's, the new rink would have ice only a few centimeters thick , and could be ready for skating just a day or two after freezing began, regardless of the outdoor conditions.

With the acquisition of a United States Hockey League franchise in August – eventually dubbed the Black Hawks – Roy Malcolm's vision of the Hippodrome as a hockey rink – and Waterloo as a hockey town – was realized again more than 30 years after slipping away.

ACKNOWLEDGEMENTS

Interesting stories are resilient. In 1954, Dick Lynes wrote an article in the *Waterloo Courier* recalling the city's fascination with hockey during the late 1920's. With the passage of two-and-a-half decades, which had included The Great Depression and World War II, not to mention the dramatic growth of other local and national sports, the details Lynes brought to his readers had been mostly forgotten. Hockey returned to the Cedar Valley eight years later and became popular again. Nearly another half-century passed with the history of the Becker-Chapman hockey team continuing to fade, now overshadowed by generations of Waterloo Black Hawks.

A worn copy of Lynes' article clipped from the paper found its way to the Waterloo Black Hawks' offices in 2009. I was curious about this team no one seemed to remember, but initially it was nothing more than a passing interest. I put the article aside in its manila envelope, and occasionally it would shuffle across my desk while I was looking for an old yearbook or a page of Hawks statistics. It wasn't until

2011, while I was writing the Black Hawks' team history, that I realized I needed to learn more about Waterloo's original team. The story of the game in this hockey-mad city wouldn't be complete if it didn't include Roy Malcolm and Earle Willey and Clarence Keyes, the first players to star on the ice here.

Much of the information about American Legion hockey in Waterloo comes from limited sources, presenting some challenges in regards to verification or alternative viewpoint. Not only was the sport new to its local chroniclers at the *Waterloo Courier*, the conventions of sportswriting in the 1920's were different. Today's sports information conveniences were non-existent even in many professional environments. These facts, coupled with the Becker-Chapman team's status as an independent club – without a league to monitor records and statistics – means that the remaining narrative within the historical source material is threadbare in some spots.

Efforts have been made to find modern information to corroborate the accounts of the 1920's. Occasionally however, these attempts to verify a particular detail or the identity of a participant have raised more questions than they have answered. Ultimately, both the author and the readers of this text can only accept as a matter of faith that, on some points, the original accounts of games and players from the era captured the facts. It is sincerely hoped that any errors or omissions in the preceding pages might be discovered and corrected by an abler hockey historian.

This project may have not been undertaken without the unwitting encouragement of both Jim Nelson of the *Waterloo-Cedar Falls Courier* and Jeff Schmidt, formerly of Iowa Public Radio. Both expressed particular interest in the few paragraphs of *Black Hawks Chronicle* which were devoted to the Becker-Chapman team. Oren Simpson of the Becker-Chapman Post generously provided the opportunity to study several volumes of the *Becker-Chapman Barrage*, which were the source for many of the details about the early days of the American Legion's local activities. Information from the Society for International Hockey Research's wonderful database and the Minnesota Historical Society's substantial newspaper archive added depth to *The Legion Team*. Thanks should also be expressed to the staff at the Waterloo Public Library for their assistance utilizing microfilm and the library's electronic databases, as well as the *Courier*'s Yvonne Keller, who was willing to scan the newspaper's archives. Catreva Manning of the Grout Museum was tremendously gracious in searching the museum's files and locating precious copies of century-old Waterloo West and Waterloo East high school yearbooks. Ken Dalgarno at the Moose Jaw Public Library pointed the way toward hard-to-find details about Clarence Keyes. Thanks too to Mary Brown for her graphic design expertise and Brandon Brockway, who has compiled a history of Waterloo in postcards and was able to locate a rare image of the Cattle Congress Hippodrome from approximately the Legion hockey era.

    The tangible product of my wife Laura's contribution to this project are the composite sketches of the Waterloo Legion's players from low-quality photos which could not have been otherwise reproduced with nearly the same quality. More importantly, she was always willing to patiently listen to my concerns and complaints as I tinkered with the manuscript. Unfailingly, she has encouraged the professional endeavors I have taken on, whether writing or broadcasting, and on the all-too-rare occasions when we can spend time together away from our jobs, she is the best friend I could ask for.

Finally, thanks to Waterloo hockey players and fans. Your enthusiasm for the game today has once again brought the Cedar Valley notoriety as a great home for the sport across the continent, and even on the other side of the world. Although hockey was played and forgotten here once, it is hard to imagine the game disappearing from the community again.

Tim Harwood
April 2013

APPENDIX – GAME-BY-GAME HISTORY

1926/27 – 2-1

Date	Opponent	Result	Score
Feb. 12	Des Moines AC Old Pals	W	13-8
Feb. 18	Le Mars Independents	W	6-5
Mar. 5	St. Paul Hook 'em Cows	L	3-6

1927/28 – 12-2

Date	Opponent	Result	Score
Dec. 17	Des Moines AC Old Pals	W	13-0
Dec. 26	Akron (IA) Independents	W	10-2
Jan. 2	St. Paul Hook 'em Cows	W	10-5
Jan. 6	Chicago Athletic Association	W	3-1
Jan. 13	South St. Paul Cowboys	W	4-0
Jan. 20	Lake Shore Athletic Club	W	4-2
Jan. 26	Fort Snelling	W	6-4
Feb. 3	American House Furnishings	W	3-2
Feb. 10	Chicago Yacht Club	W	4-0
Feb. 15	Winnipeg Buffaloes	W	2-1
Feb. 17	Winnipeg Buffaloes	W	4-1
Feb. 20	Winnipeg Buffaloes	L	0-3
Feb. 28	Kansas City Pla-Mors	L	1-6
Mar. 2	Fort Snelling	W	8-1

1928/29 – 8-4

Date	Opponent	Result	Score
Dec. 25	3M	L	2-5
Jan. 1	W.D. Forshay	W	3-2
Jan. 4	Armour Packers	W	6-3
Jan. 11	St. Mary's College	W	3-1
Jan. 18	Chicago Athletic Association	L	3-4
Jan. 26	Fort Snelling	W	2-1
Feb. 1	Chicago College of Osteopathy	W	9-1
Feb. 6	Winnipeg Maple Leafs	W	2-1
Feb. 8	Winnipeg Maple Leafs	L	2-5
Feb. 11	Winnipeg Maple Leafs	L	1-2
Feb. 20	3M	W	5-4
Mar. 8	Fort Snelling	W	8-4

The Legion Team

1929/30 – 8-3-2

Date	Opponent	Result	Score
Dec. 25	3M	L	2-3
Jan. 1	Janesville (WI) Independents	W	2-1
Jan. 5	Van Paper Company	L	1-3
Jan. 12	St. Mary's College	W	4-3
Jan. 19	Minnesota Wanderers	W	6-2
Jan. 24	St. Mary's College	T	1-1
Jan. 26	St. Mary's College	T	2-2
Jan. 31	Rogers Park	W	5-2
Feb. 2	Rogers Park	W	7-1
Feb. 7	Northern Pacific Railway	W	9-1
Feb. 9	Northern Pacific Railway	W	5-2
Feb. 14	St. Mary's College	W	1-0
Feb. 16	St. Mary's College	L	1-2

www.ingramcontent.com/pod-product-compliance
Lightning Source LLC
Chambersburg PA
CBHW061950070426
42450CB00007BA/1174